Some Kind of *love*

Memoirs of Hope and Redemption in Liberia, West Africa

BY GLORIA MILLER | PHOTOGRAPHS BY MARCUS WILLEY

© 2013 by TGS International, a wholly owned subsidiary of Christian Aid Ministries, Berlin, Ohio.

All rights reserved. No part of this book may be distributed, uploaded, used, reproduced, or stored in any retrieval system, in any form or by any means, electronic or mechanical, without written permission from the publisher except for brief quotations embodied in critical articles and reviews.

ISBN: 978-1-939084-38-5

Printed in South Korea.

Published by:
TGS International
P.O. Box 355, Berlin, OH 44610 USA
Phone 330.893.4828 · 330.893.2305
www.tgsinternational.com

Julia Hunsberger, Design and Layout
Sherilyn Yoder, Editor

Gloria Miller, Author
Marcus Willey, Photographer (unless noted below)
    Joe Byler: pg. 54 (top left)
    Morris Lapp: pg. 54 (bottom right)
    Gloria Miller: pg. 35, pg. 84, pg. 87

DEDICATION

FOR THE CHILDREN of Liberia, West Africa—the ones who taught me that filth, disease, and poverty fade in comparison to redemption, hope, and love. Bridging cultures and continents, your love created a space in my heart that I didn't know existed. Without you there would be no stories.

CONTENTS

Preface VII

Acknowledgments X

1. Just Remember, No Tears 3
2. Some Kind of Love 5
3. Scars on Her Heart 12
4. Five Minutes and a Red Plastic Cup 18
5. The Absence of Love 25
6. Memories of Terror 29
7. Two Weeks and One Can 35
8. Simple Thanksgiving 39
9. He Will Redeem Them 42
10. Pictures of Hope 47
11. Not Even a Sparrow 53

12. What I Learned in a West African Village 59

13. Two Babies and the Breath of Life 65

14. Tell the Truth 69

15. Rebecca's Gifts 75

16. One Kiss 85

17. Inside the Bamboo Walls 91

18. A Reason to Smile Again 99

19. A Fearful Thing 103

20. A Different Ending 109

Appendix: Reports on Selected Needs in Liberia 117

    An Educational Vision 119

    An Axe, a Cutlass, and a Paring Knife 123

    A Bundle Can Save a Baby's Life 131

PREFACE

IN 2010 I began working with Christian Aid Ministries in Liberia, West Africa. Christian Aid's base in Liberia supplies clinics and hospitals with desperately needed medicine and other supplies, assists orphanages and vulnerable children with food and schooling, provides food for widows and the elderly, and aids farmers with tools and seeds. My job as secretary included printing delivery lists for the supplies leaving the warehouse, recording and updating orphan profiles, checking inventory, making copies for our national staff, and much more. With the stream of people in and out of my office every day, I had the opportunity to meet some of those who came to CAM for help and to hear their stories.

During my time in Liberia, I emailed my family and friends with chronicles of the stories I encountered. In this book, I have compiled those emails plus other stories. The result is a picture of my two and a half years there and of the people who touched my life.

Liberia was founded by freed American and Caribbean slaves, but the descendants of these freed slaves make up only 5 percent of the population. Indigenous Africans make up the majority of the population. They are divided into sixteen tribes, three of which are mentioned in this book: Kpelle, Bassa, and Gio. As is common throughout Africa, tribal allegiance runs deep in Liberia. Each tribe speaks its own native dialect, which causes distance between the tribes.

Most Liberians can speak English, which is taught in schools, but it differs from the North American version. Words are repeated or "o" is added to the end for extra emphasis. Something may be *small small* or *fine-o*. Different terms for our English words are used as well. For example, the rice may be *finished* instead of *all gone*, the driver may *carry* you instead of *drive*, *dress* means *to move*, and *trying small small* actually means *to try hard*. Although the Liberian language may sound a bit odd or simplistic to the unaccustomed American ear, I have tried to keep some of its distinct African flavor in the stories of this book.

At one time, Liberia was one of the most prosperous African nations. The minority Americo-Liberians, descendants of the freed slaves, ruled the government. But the seeds of a ruinous civil war began in 1980 when Samuel Doe carried out a military coup against President Tolbert, publically executing him and thirteen of his aides. The People's Redemption Council, headed by Doe, assumed full power. An indigenous Liberian from the Krahn tribe, Doe had accomplished his goal of removing the Americo-Liberians from power. Doe's regime continued semi-peacefully until 1989, when the National Patriotic Front of Liberia (NPFL) rose up against the government. Led by Charles Taylor, a former official in Doe's government, the uprising was motivated by ethnic conflicts. Taylor's group targeted Doe's Krahn tribe as well as a people group called the Mandingos. Primarily Muslim, the Mandingos were not recognized as a tribe by most Liberians, since the majority of Liberians consider themselves "Christian."

Years of chaotic, sporadic fighting ensued. In 1997, Charles Taylor won the presidential election, but stability remained elusive. A group of rebels united and began anti-government fighting. In 2003 the rebels reached Monrovia, the capital of Liberia, and one of the worst civil wars in history climaxed. Hemmed in by rebels and pressured by international governments to resign from his reign of terror, Taylor went into exile in Nigeria.

This ended the war, and Liberia was at peace. But peace had not come without heavy cost. Since more than 200,000 people were killed in the war, nearly every person had lost a mother, father, sister, brother, child, aunt, or uncle. Thousands were displaced. The economy and infrastructure had been shattered; some say the civil war set Liberia back seventy-five years. Reeling from the terrible price of war, the people of Liberia still struggle to rebuild their lives.

Many more things give Liberia its own cultural flair, but I hope the few facts mentioned will help you to better understand the people and happenings in this book. Maybe you, too, can have a glimpse of God's hope and redemption working to change the hearts of many who never before experienced love. This book is not just about starving and malnourished children—it is about God and His powerful love. *Some kind of love!*

Liberia Profile; BBC © 2012

Liberia; CIA; The World Factbook © 2012

ACKNOWLEDGMENTS

MY FAMILY—Mom, Dad, Conrad, Julia, Austin, CJ, and Violet. Thank you for listening to my dreams. Even when you laughed at all my wild ideas, I knew that you believed in me, and that made all the difference. A special thanks to Julia, for the hours spent brainstorming with me, designing this book, reading my mind, and knowing what I wanted even when I didn't myself. Your prayers as a family were behind me, and they are what held me. I am so proud to call you my family. I love you all.

MY FRIENDS—Melody, Wesley, and Melissa. Thank you for pouring your time and hearts into this book and my life. Melody, thanks for roughing it with me in the villages of Africa. Wesley, thanks for the late night Skype conversations, emails, and for always praying for me. Melissa, thanks for the great talks and brewing Turkish coffee for me when the deadline crunch hit hard. You are the best friends I could ask for.

THE EXPAT TEAM (foreigners living in Liberia) at Tower Hill—you encouraged me to write this book, you challenged me to set my goals higher, and you pushed me to step out of my comfort zone. Without you, this book would never have been a reality. And since these stories ultimately reflect what God is doing through Christian Aid Ministries in Liberia, I pray I portrayed an accurate picture of our team. Thank you for all the advice, the wisdom, and the wiped-away tears and shared laughter. Most of all, thank you for being my friends and an extension of my family.

MY LIBERIAN FRIENDS—Tamba, David, Anthony, Akin, Toney, Tracie, Holder, Varney, Andrew, and Marvin, just to name a few. Thank you, Tamba, for driving me around Monrovia; David, for helping me with Elisha's story; Anthony, for Darius' story; Toney, for taking me all the way to Ganta; Tracie—the story "One Kiss" is all because of you; Andrew, for teaching me words from the Bassa dialect; Marvin, for sharing your passion for the children of Liberia with me. And to all the other Tower Hill staff, I loved being your secretary. God be with you all.

JESUS—my best Friend. You are sure and unchanging when nothing stays the same. So many people have walked in and out of my life, but you are always there, through every tough time. I love you more than life and breath. Thank you for doing more for me than I could ever dream, and thank you that every day you are changing me to what you want me to be. Every word, every story, is for you.

CHAPTER ONE
JUST REMEMBER, NO TEARS

MIA AND I always had a special bond. I was her first babysitter, and she was my first child to babysit. She was born when I was thirteen years old, and we became the best of friends even when she was just a tiny baby. We read books for hours on the porch swing and took four-wheeler rides in the meadows. Best friends, Mia and me. When you're an awkward teenager, a toddler is safer than girls your own age.

Mia and I loved the stories we read while suspended on the wicker swing. Our favorite one was the story of a little girl who lived back in the pioneer days. In her younger years, she played doll and rode horses like a normal girl. Then she grew up. After she got married, she climbed into a covered wagon with her new husband to explore the wild, untamed West. When she said goodbye to her family, she knew she would most likely never see them again. As she left, she looked back at them and said, "Just remember, no tears."

And her dad said, "That's right, no tears." But as the wagon rolled away, he wiped tears from his eyes.

For some reason we just loved that story, and we read it over and over. Then things changed. The long summer days of Schwan's popsicles and books and the porch swing faded into the past, replaced for me by high school graduation and a new job; for her by first grade and two baby brothers.

Of the changes that followed in my life, the biggest one came when I was twenty years old: leaving home to go to Africa. It wasn't just Mia I was leaving, but my whole family—my brothers, my sisters, and my parents.

I left for Africa, an unknown place for an unknown amount of time.

That day at the airport, I recognized that when close families say goodbye to each other, several patterns tend to emerge. Brothers slap shoulders and give a sort of pounding hug, as if anything else would show too much tenderness or emotion. But you know it's there.

Sisters say goodbye in a way that only sisters can, with emotion that comes from years of understanding each other in a way no one else does.

Dads have a sudden interest in the flight schedule and TSA agents and luggage weights and try not to look you in the eye. Then they finally say, "Let's get it over with," and give you a giant hug and tell you to take care.

Moms squeeze you hard, put a head on your shoulder, and shut their eyes to hold back tears born from years of feeding, loving, and caring. Then just before you leave, they give you one more hug.

I noticed these common patterns because I glanced over at a fellow passenger who was leaving in army fatigues. His family surrounded him and said their goodbyes in the same way my family was saying theirs, right down to the second last-minute hug from his mom.

It's called leaving with a whole lot of love.

As I turned my back and walked through security, it was hard to leave. But somehow I felt secure and safe, knowing the love of my family was supporting me.

For the first forty days, my family and close relatives sent a card for me to open each day. Here's what Mia's card said:

Dear Gloria,

It's me, Mia. I hope you have a good time. I know it will be hard. Just remember you are welcome back home every day. And know you are loved. I do hope you are OK.

And just remember, no tears.

Love,

Mia

The "no tears" part—well, when I left the United States, it was pouring rain as I walked into that airplane in Chicago. I remember looking out the big glass airport windows, matching the rain by crying my eyes out, and thinking to myself, *I'm leaving, and I'm crying. Never mind the "no tears."* I used my cell phone one last time. I talked to my mom and cried. And she cried. The last person I talked to was my dad. And he was crying.

Deep inside I knew the tears meant something—they meant I was well-loved.

My aunt, who was a missionary in Central and South America for nine years, told me before I left, "Gloria, you'll leave America crying, and someday you'll leave Africa crying."

Whatever, I thought those first months in Africa. *I sure won't ever cry when I leave this place.*

But now I know I will. One year or ten years, a lot of changes happen. Love grows—and now I know I'll leave Africa, crying.

Because of some kind of love.

CHAPTER TWO
SOME KIND OF LOVE

THIS STORY HOLDS a special place in my heart because I think it's where this book was born. And since this story marks the birth of this book, it deserves a background explanation.

I had been serving in Liberia for a year. I left home a young twenty years old. It was a tough year—a year with four bouts of malaria, more than twice that many of homesickness, and some huge cultural learning curves. After my first year, I was privileged to go home for a three-week furlough, which included my sister's wedding. To say I was excited would be an understatement—I mean, I was going home!

But just before I went home, the day before I got on the airplane, something happened. I met Joshua William. And even though I was so excited about going home, I found myself thinking of Joshua while curled up in my seat on the airplane. I found myself writing his story in a coffee shop during my layover in Brussels, and looking at his picture again and again during my twenty hours of travel. On the final flight into my homeland of Ohio, I turned my face to the window to hide my tears, which were attracting some curious glances from the stewardess and my neighbors across the aisle. I was a different person from the twenty-year-old who had left home a year before, and Joshua was the epitome of how West Africa had changed my life.

The story stayed with me through my whole furlough. One day I was in the computer center at Staples receiving emails on my laptop. The IT man helping me was one of my dad's old friends. I stood with my dad and this man at the Staples computer center as emails flowed into my inbox, seeing that a few were from Liberia.

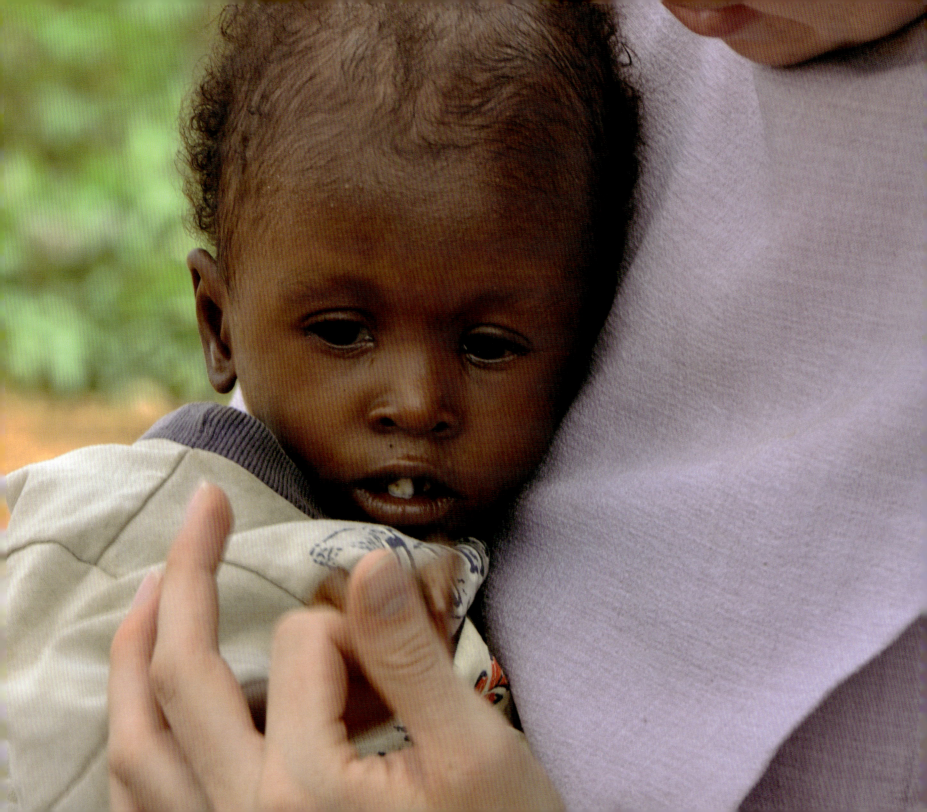

I read those on the spot. When I came to an update on how Joshua was doing, I started crying. Even though I hadn't said a word, the IT man turned to my dad and said, "Your daughter—look at her. Her heart's in Africa."

We first heard about Joshua when Brother Dirkson came to CAM's office and told us there was a very malnourished child living right next to the new house he was building.

"All right, let's go find them and I'll see for myself," Marcus, CAM's medicine program director, said. When we got to the dwelling, we found a tiny child lying on a mat in front of a shack with a tin zinc roof held down with rocks.

Joshua was one and a half years old, yet his spindly legs could not hold his little body. His face showed absolutely no expression, and his eyes seemed to have a hard time focusing on anything.

"What's wrong with him?" we asked Ma Esther, his grandma.

The "ole ma" (elderly lady) just shook her head and sighed, "I don't know."

"Who is the child's father?"

"Well, that's my son," was her reply. "But I can't see him (he doesn't come around) and I don't know where he is. My husband died in 1994."

We learned that her son, Joshua Sr., was twenty-four years old. He abandoned Joshua's mother after the baby was born. When Joshua was six months old, his mother decided she did not want the responsibility of her child either. So, as Ma Esther said, "She just dashed the child on me and left." Grimly, I thought of how often that happens in Liberia. The boyfriend abandons his girlfriend after

SOME KIND OF LOVE | 7

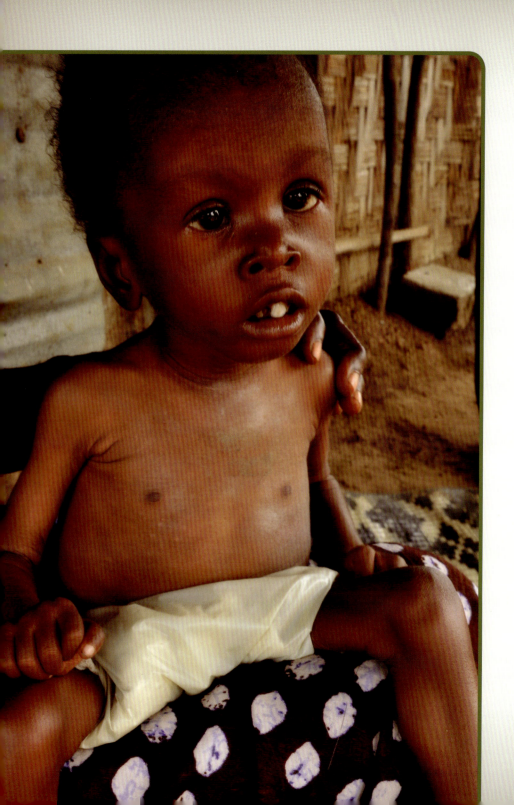

she delivers his baby, and many times the young mother rejects the burden of raising a child alone. She decides to leave her baby with a relative, deserting the child for the "good life."

We gave Ma Esther four boxes of Herbalife (nutritional drink) and showed her how to prepare it. After we left, Brother Dirkson quoted Isaiah 49:15: "Can a woman forget her sucking child, that she should not have compassion on the son of her womb?" But this is the situation in which many children find themselves in Liberia.

Only three days after Joshua took his first drink of Herbalife, Marcus, Brother Dirkson, and I visited him again. When we arrived, we found Joshua lying on the same mat beside the shack.

Ma Esther came up to greet us right away, leaving her work in the garden and carrying a scratching hoe. She was dressed in typical Liberian style for an ole ma, with her head tie and *lapa* (versatile piece of fabric used as a skirt, baby carrier, potholder, etc.).

Ma Esther has a beautiful garden. While she showed Marcus and Brother Dirkson her sweet potatoes, okra, cassava, sugar cane, and saw-saw (soursop) tree, I held Joshua and talked to him.

I loved holding him. He didn't talk and he didn't cry, but every so often he would let out a pitiful little squeak. Almost without thinking about it, I found myself saying, "Look, you need to grow to be a strong boy, a strong man. Can you hold my hand?"

Amazingly, he could. Well, his tiny fingers could grasp my little finger. And one time, just once, he put one hand on my shoulder and one on my arm and just looked at me. When he held my finger and touched my shoulder and arm, it occurred to me those were the only real voluntary movements Joshua made. And when I say he looked at me—well, his look was not the normal look of a 1½-year-old. Just like the first visit, his eyes didn't focus, and his skin was like thinly stretched leather over long, scrawny bones.

But we were amazed at the difference only three days had made—Joshua's eyes already focused a tiny bit better, and he had a little color in his cheeks. Brother Dirkson agreed and said, "The man, he just needs love. Some kind of love."

I didn't want to leave my baby Joshua. And here I catch myself saying "baby." Wait—normally, a child nearly two years old is not a baby. But what is normal?

Some say normal is just a setting on your dryer. And maybe that has a grain of truth. Life is not normal; life is not fair. In spite of life-saving nutrition, Joshua will probably never develop quite normally.

SOME KIND OF LOVE | 9

But that doesn't mean his life doesn't matter. It doesn't mean I can ignore his needs. I can still try to make life better for him, and I can love him with God's love.

As I flew thousands of miles away back to my home in America, I could picture myself in another place. Huddling under a blanket on seat 28K, I imagined I was sitting on a crude wooden bench in the hot African sun, shaded by a dilapidated hut with a corrugated roof held down by about twenty rocks. I heard little chicks peeping as they scurried after their mother hen scratching in the dirt. I saw Ma Esther showing Marcus and Brother Dirkson her vegetable garden. And when I closed my eyes, I could almost feel something in my arms—a tiny child snuggled right up against me, saying nothing, but letting out a pathetic little cry every so often. His eyes were barely focusing, but he could smile just a bit. He was hanging onto my little finger. And then I realized that Joshua didn't just wrap his fingers around mine, but he wrapped them all the way around my heart.

Maybe Joshua is not normal and never will be. But I think I am realizing the abnormal things in life, the things that cause us pain in the core of our being, create more space in our hearts. Space for, as we say in Liberia, "some kind of love." And maybe—just maybe—that is better than normal.

> The things that cause us pain in the core of our being, create more space in our hearts. Space for, as we say in Liberia, some kind of love.

CHAPTER THREE
SCARS ON HER HEART

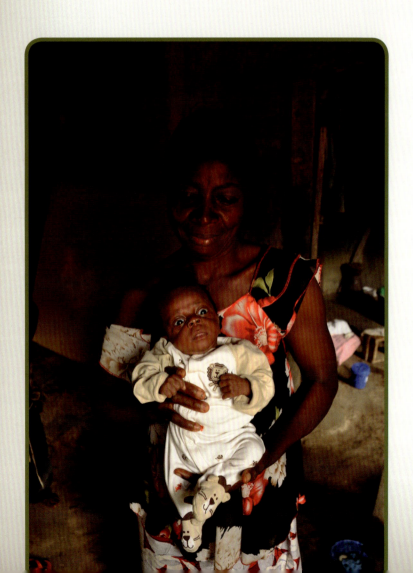

SHE MET US at the door, cradling a baby in her arms. Her house on Peace Island was only a tiny room—a shack, really. Inside hung two mosquito nets for sleeping. One had a bed under it, but the other net covered just a few blankets to protect the children from the hard dirt floor at night. The roof leaked, so the nights were likely wet and miserable during this long rainy season. You could see through cracks in the house walls. On the porch, screened in by pink and white rice bags sewn together, sat a little boy grinning widely at us while fiddling around with his toy—a worn out, rusty stapler.

She sat down and told us her story.

My name is Teetee. Teetee Weedor.

When I was eight years old, I lived in the small city of Ganta, just south of the Guinea border. I lived with my mother and my little sister Josephine, who was four. One day when I came home from school, Josephine and I were alone in the yard because Mama was out selling market goods to make a few dollars. That's when we heard it—gunshots. Liberia's awful civil war had come to our area. We just ran, terrified. We ran with all the other people. We left Mama behind and ran and ran. We ran toward the Guinea border.

When we crossed the border, a Guinea soldier took us under his wing. He took us far, far from Liberia, all the way through Guinea and ending near the border of the West African country of Senegal.

The Guinea man, who was Muslim, took care of us girls. I grew up in his hand, and I think I might even have trusted him. He was old, much older than me. When he first took me, he was forty-two years old.

But then everything changed. When I got older and became a woman, he did unspeakable things to me. I can't even say. I was seventeen years old when I gave birth to Lavea, my baby girl. The man was fifty-one years old.

My son Michael was born next, when I was twenty. The man said it was too long between births. Muslim women are supposed to bear a child every year. Since I didn't, he beat me. He beat my shoulders, my back, and my legs with his belt. Or sometimes he hit my face with the palm of his hands. I never knew what would bring a beating—sometimes if I just broke a dish, he would beat me.

One horrible, awful day, he broke my leg. The pain was too much. I wanted to leave and go back to Liberia. But the man always said I must leave my children with him; I could not take them back with me. I couldn't bear to part with them. They were my own flesh and blood; I loved them. So I endured—and stayed.

Kado, my little frisky son, was born when I was twenty-three years old.

It bothered me that I couldn't take my children to church. The man forced me to go to a Muslim mosque. I went only because he forced me to go.

My sister Josephine got involved with a boyfriend and became pregnant. Her time came too early. We were far from a clinic, and she had her baby at home. She named him Emanuel. It means "God with us."

But Josephine died the same day that Emanuel was born. He was born nearly three months early.

And the man we lived with said Emanuel was as good as dead, because he was so tiny. He didn't want the responsibility of a struggling baby. And he didn't want me anymore, or our children. He wanted to marry a woman from his own tribe. So he just trashed me and all the children.

We were free to go. But more than free, we were helpless and

14 | SOME KIND OF LOVE

desperate. I had a twelve-year-old daughter, a nine-year-old son, a five-year-old son, and my sister's almost-dead baby. And I had discovered two months earlier that I was expecting again.

God sent a kind woman to talk to me. She said she had a sister who lived in Monrovia, Liberia. Her sister had a house I could live in. She encouraged me to go back to Liberia, my home. So I went.

We loaded all our things on the back of a big truck, all three of my children and I, and baby Emanuel. We traveled from the Senegal/Guinea border to Monrovia. It took us five days to reach Monrovia. The rough roads and crowded truck were not easy. My children cried and cried. But there was no other way for us—the taxi car was too expensive.

I came to Monrovia and found this place, a little hut on Peace Island. But I still had a hard time. Emanuel had me so worried. He couldn't even grow. He cried and cried. I had no money to buy milk for him, so I fed him what I could: [a powdered form of] glucose and mineral water.

I needed to support my family, so to make a little money, I plaited hair. Weaving hair paid more, but it took too long—two hours at a time. With a baby, three children, and another baby on the way, I just couldn't do it. So I plaited hair, because it didn't take as long and I could care for Emanuel better. But I made only a little money. And it was never enough for our needs.

One day I just started to cry. I thought Emanuel was going to die, just like my little sister Josephine.

A woman saw me crying and said, "Fine girl, what's wrong?"

I said, "Look here, my sister's baby. She died. And this boy, he just getting too small now, his stomach just growing. I think he coming to die."

The kind woman gave me money—she gave me 10 USD. And I heard that Christian Aid Ministries was giving milk to malnourished babies. So I took a taxi car to Christian Aid Ministries at Tower Hill. This was the first time I ever heard about them.

At Christian Aid Ministries, they listened to my story. They gave me milk for nothing. They held Emanuel and took his picture. And they even said I could come back when the milk is finished and get more.

Now the best part of my story is that Emanuel is doing better. He is still small, too small, but every week I see he is growing a little.

I went to Ganta, my home, for the first time since I came back to Liberia. It was a long drive, about five hours on bad roads.

I met my mother there. It was hard, because it was too long since I had last seen her. But I think I will go to live with her now. Because when my time comes, when the pain grabs me, then my mother will hold my hand and help me. And I won't be alone when my baby is born.

I left Kado with my mother when I came back here, because I knew I was going back soon. She wanted to keep Emanuel too, but I said, "No, I am the one that got feeling for Emanuel, and it was Josephine and me that got caught in hard times together, in the war and in Guinea." So I kept him.

And tomorrow, right after church service, we are going to Ganta, my children and I. I will go during the day, because I don't want to travel with my children at night. The place I'm going, I don't know the area, but I'm in God's hands. God can help me. I know He can.

Before we left, we prayed for Teetee. I put my arms around her while Marcus prayed. As I buried my face in her shoulder, I smelled her musty denim jacket—someone else's castoff clothing. I heard a rooster crowing in the background, behind her pathetic, falling-apart shack. I felt Emanuel pressed gently between us, and I heard him whimpering.

I realized that Teetee had entrusted us with her life story. She had lifted her *lapa* and shown us the ugly scar from the beating that broke her leg. Her life lay open before us.

Teetee had revealed something far deeper as well— the awful abuse, rejection, and pain . . . the scars on her heart. Scars so deep, so painful, that only Jesus and His unconditional love can heal them. And it is my prayer that He will—that Teetee will let His love heal the scars on her heart.

I have loved thee with an everlasting love: therefore with lovingkindness have I drawn thee.
—JEREMIAH 31:3

> **Scars so deep, so painful, that only Jesus and His unconditional love can heal them.**

16 | SOME KIND OF LOVE

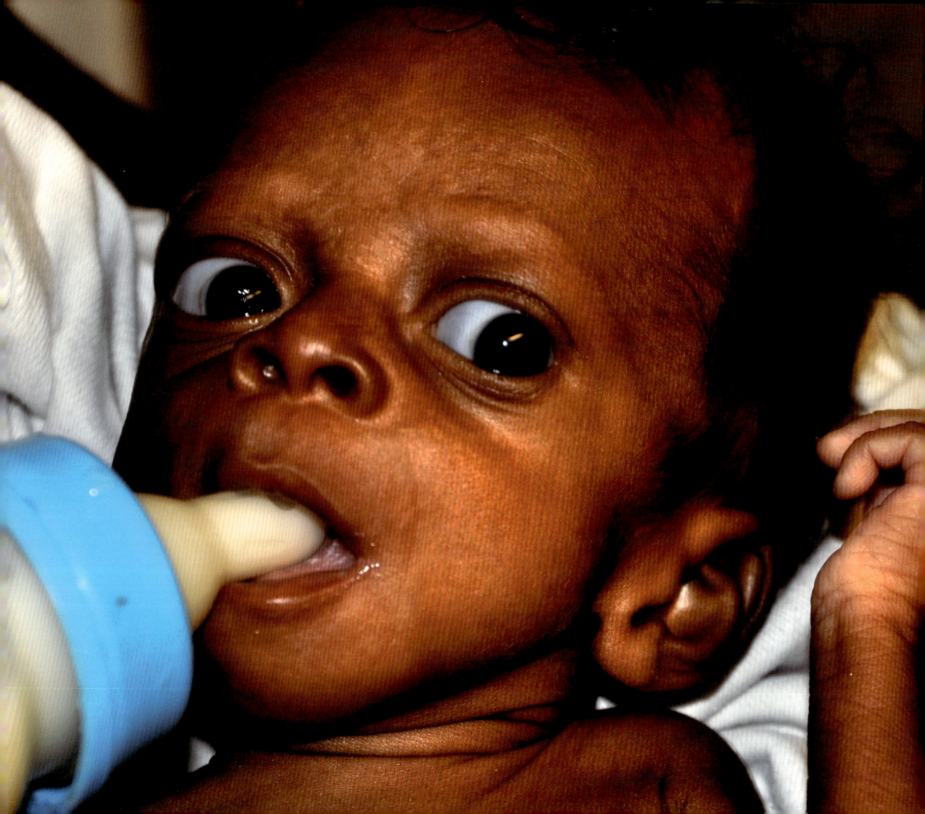

CHAPTER FOUR
FIVE MINUTES AND A RED PLASTIC CUP

IT WAS A typical Monday morning at Tower Hill. Lots of people were waiting to see the bossman, hoping for help in the form of a food box or zinc for their roofs. It was rainy season, and the rain was giving them a hard time. The biweekly orphan program meeting was being held, which meant eight administrators needed money for school fees and all sorts of other things for the orphans in their districts. The agriculture team was preparing to go deep in the bush to Rivercess County for distribution, so all of their preparations were being made. We were starting with the month's medical delivery, so the warehouse staff members were busy loading the Land Cruiser to take medicines to clinics. All morning long, employees came in and out of my office, needing anything from paper clips to inventory counts to copies of orphan profiles.

It was in the middle of this that Marcus called me. "Gloria, I'm sending a lady with a little boy over to you to interview."

"Okay," I said. (We have a saying here: *Be flexible or miserable*. I try to choose the former!) "Do you want me to do a delivery note for her?"

"Not yet," he said. "I'll be over soon."

So I tried to clear a spot on my desk, get Jimmy's delivery notes printed and stamped, and figure out an orphan profile number for Joe before she came.

She came in—a typical ole ma in Liberia, with *lapa* and head tie, the bright colors contrasting against her dark, weathered skin—and she was smiling as though everything was fine. Then she untied a bundle from her back.

A tiny, malnourished boy. He already had teeth, and from his features I guessed he was about one year old. She held him in her arms and sat in the chair beside me. And I tried to interview her and dig for her story.

But the little boy cried. And cried. Desperately, seriously, he cried.

I tried to communicate with the ole ma, Siatta Tamba. She was smiling and as friendly as could be, but she really could not speak English well. Because she was from Lofa County, she spoke the African dialect known as Gezee. "My English not too well!" Siatta kept saying. But with the help of a paper she had carried over from Marcus, on which he had written what he found out about the story, I got the sketchy details of her story and why she was here.

The little boy, Darius Tamba, was her grandson. She originated from Foya, Lofa County, which is a full day's journey by taxi car from Tower Hill. In Liberia, a taxi car is a beat-up little yellow machine sporting a bumper sticker with a random saying like "God's Divine Favor" on the back—not exactly what I would call a dependable ride.

Back to Siatta. Her son got married and lived

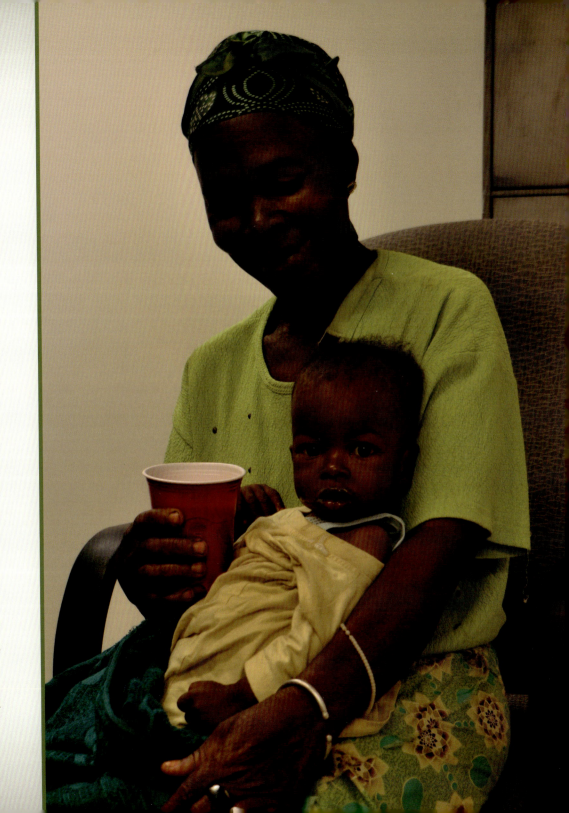

in Grand Bassa County, not far away from Tower Hill. But Siatta's daughter-in-law got sick and died. Siatta's son sent for her to come get her little grandson and care for him. So she did, coming all the way from Foya. "Let the son's ma carry the baby," she said. And she took him with her to Foya to care for him.

But only two weeks later, Siatta's son also got sick and died. Siatta went back to Grand Bassa County for the burial. Now she and Darius were "stopping" (living for a while) with a friend in Scheiffelin.

With no money, far from her own tribe and people, and with a language barrier even in her own country, Siatta struggled to eke out a living. Back in Lofa, many of her family and friends had died during the war. The few remaining struggled to survive as well, so Siatta wouldn't get much help from there to support her little grandson.

Because of these circumstances, desperate little Darius was now sitting on his grandma's lap in my office at Tower Hill, which was only a five-minute drive from Scheiffelin. "The boy and myself, we suffering!" Siatta said. "We been here in Scheiffelin now for three days. Back in Foya I got country rice (locally grown rice) I would make and give to Darius, but here no food, no family. No help."

Obviously, country rice is not what a one-year-old boy needs, but it is better than nothing—which was the problem now. Well, Siatta had given him water. But that is same as nothing. This was Monday, and the last time they ate was Sunday morning. Siatta looked all right, but Darius was not okay. It's impossible to describe how his eyes looked to me. They looked like the eyes of a little boy who has experienced too much suffering, pain, and now hunger. Orphaned and malnourished, the baby in front of me was a heartrending spectacle.

It seemed like forever until Marcus came, although in reality it was no more than five minutes. Hearing Darius' heartbreaking cries was almost too much for me to handle. Siatta tried so hard to comfort him. "Na mind, na mind" (Never mind, it's okay), she kept saying. "Here, take this," and she

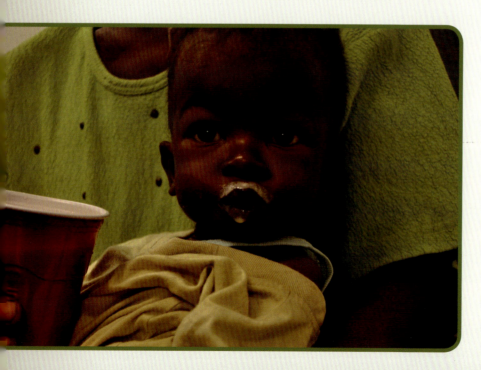

stuffed a crumpled, dirty 20 LD (Liberian Dollars) bill into his hand. "See, one man gave me this while I was here waiting, and when we finished, we will leave to the village and I will try to buy some bread for you. Na mind, na mind."

But Darius continued to cry.

Marcus brought two boxes of Herbalife nutritional drink mix into my office and set them on my desk. He combined a packet of the mix with water in a red plastic cup and gave it to Darius. The child drank it eagerly, almost like a hungry dog or cat would lap up milk. In just a few moments he wore a big milk mustache and an even bigger grin that went all the way to his eyes. His shrunken stomach could handle only a little bit of milk. Not more than an inch of the liquid in the red plastic cup disappeared, but it was enough. Enough for him to grin and to be alert when we talked to him. In just a few minutes, he stole my heart.

Darius and Siatta left, but I can't forget them. Quite realistically, I believe we can say Darius' life was saved. So many malnourished children fall prey to malaria or pneumonia and die from these preventable diseases. By the look in Darius' eyes and the sound of his cries, we could tell he could have become one of these tragic cases. But we were able to be messengers of God's grace to Darius through a few tiny measures.

Five minutes that Monday morning—the time it takes to scan a document, type a letter, or make a pot of coffee for the office. One red plastic cup—the kind that holds frothy root beer floats or southern iced tea at a picnic. But that Monday morning it held Herbalife nutritional milk. Not fancy, not much, but that morning it meant everything to Darius.

In the following months, Siatta came to our office for more milk, and we loved seeing Darius' health drastically improve as he began to walk and talk. He could finally eat and play just like little boys should. One day when Siatta brought him to the office for a visit and more milk, she said, "That day, we can't forget it! You did it for my boy."

I think it is the little things that change our lives too. The small but significant moments are life-giving. They are the things we can't—and shouldn't—forget.

> I think it is the **little things** that change our lives too. The small but significant moments are life-giving. They are the things we can't—and shouldn't—forget.

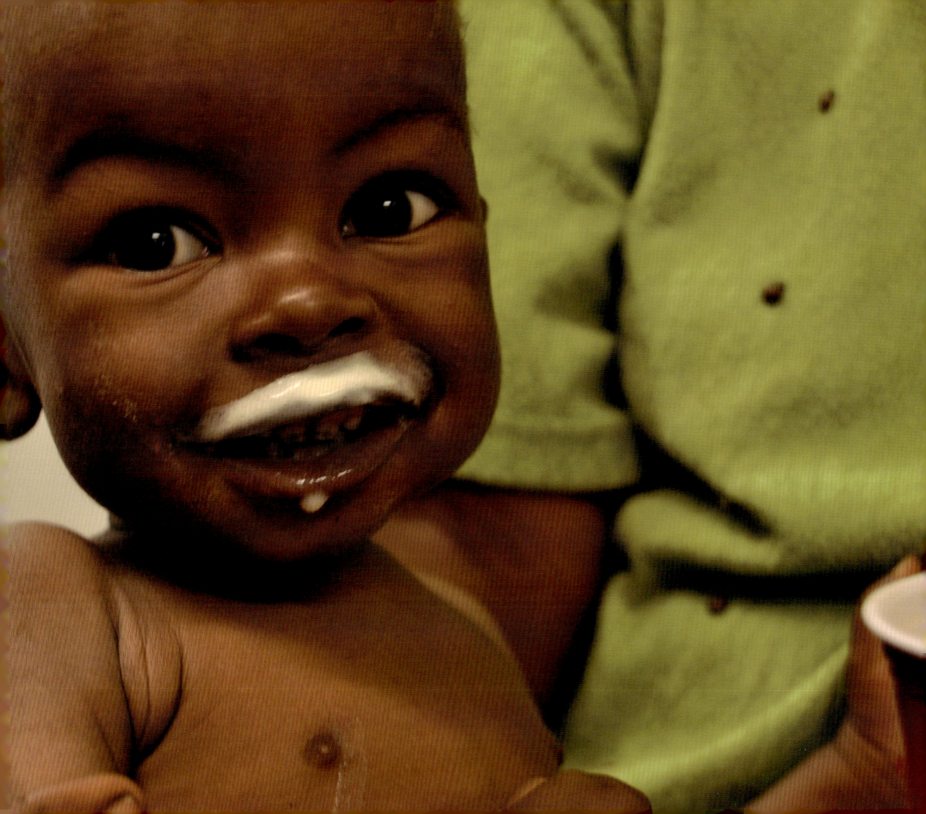

CHAPTER FIVE
THE ABSENCE OF LOVE

IT'S MORBID. The absence of love—and the image that is forever burned on my heart and soul.

Godsgift lives right beside Darius, the little boy in "Five Minutes and a Red Plastic Cup." But while Darius lives in a decrepit shack, Godsgift was sitting in a little chair on the porch of a nice concrete house when we met him.

It's funny how two years earlier I would never have called the house nice. But I do now. By Liberian standards, it is upscale. Made of concrete, freshly whitewashed, and big, it has a porch and an adequate floor covering inside.

Two years earlier I would also never have noticed that this was a party house. But I did today because of the big case of bottles that said "Monrovia Brewery" on the side, and the coolers and ice chest inside the house.

At nearly two years of age, Godsgift was desperately malnourished. The story is that his mother was mentally unstable and did not breast-feed him; consequently, he became severely ill.

Godsgift was staying with his auntie, who had a commanding spirit about her. She was dressed in a fine red suit and had hair attachments. She told us she was a missionary, a statement we took with a grain of salt.

She got chairs for us, and we sat on the porch. Marcus began asking her questions about the boy. After a short time of answering questions, she started giving orders to Godsgift. She told him to stand up, I suppose because she wanted us to see him standing. But when he just stayed sitting, her tone of voice became demanding. "Stand up!" she told him, ignoring his apparent inability to do so. She turned to us and said, "When I talk to him, he can fight to do it." She meant that he could do her bidding if he'd put forth enough effort.

She tried to force him to stand up, but his spindly legs couldn't even hold his own weight, and he started to cry. She finally gave him a stick to hold on to; somehow that was supposed to help him stand. But he still couldn't stand alone. He was just too weak. Finally she helped him hold onto the cooler beside his chair, and he stood that way.

I still don't know what she wanted to prove by getting him to stand for us. Marcus told her to please let him sit down, so she let him sit on his little chair again. The entire time, Godsgift was crying—heart-wrenching cries that came from deep inside his body.

And then something else happened. I was horrified by what I saw, and I looked away and then looked again to make sure it was true. Blood was seeping out of the corners of his mouth.

"Marcus," I said, "look, he's bleeding!"

He had seen it too. "So why is the boy bleeding?" he asked the auntie.

"That sore that caused it. Sore in his stomach."

She picked up an old bottle from a nearby table and poured some

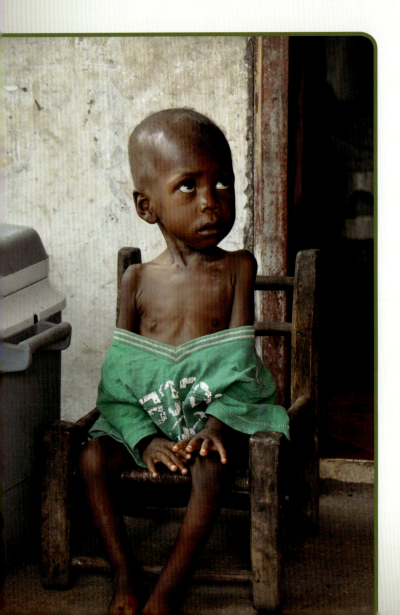

> Even if my little friend got Herbalife, it wouldn't heal him completely. It might heal his body, but it wouldn't heal the part inside him that is crying out for **just one drink of love.**

of the substance into the cap and gave it to him. Then she took his oversized green shirt and wiped the blood from the corners of his mouth.

Every once in a while, Godsgift would lift a filthy hand to his running nose and try to wipe it, but he just smeared it all up. It was a mess.

Eventually the auntie left, after Marcus told her how to prepare the Herbalife nutritional milk he had brought for Godsgift. We stayed on the porch for a little while longer, and I went over to the forlorn boy and sat on the same cooler that he had been holding onto earlier for support. I held out my hand to him, and he grabbed hold of my finger and held on to it.

After a little while, I pulled my hand away and we left. But when I walked away across that sandy soil, I just couldn't pull my heart away. I came home and kept thinking about him while I ate my late lunch of cold rice and potato greens. Then Dorothy stopped by my office where I was trying to focus on my work, and I told her about Godsgift.

Dorothy said, "You know, Gloria, it's not the first time there's been a very malnourished child in that area."

"I know," I said. We read each other's thoughts. Besides Darius, there had been another malnourished baby in that area about a year ago. We had gotten there too late for him. Since he hadn't been cared for well and hadn't gotten nutritional milk in time, he had died.

But this was another child and a different time. Maybe his auntie would give him the Herbalife, and he would get better. I hoped so. But I thought that even if my little friend got Herbalife, it wouldn't heal him completely. It might heal his body, but it wouldn't heal the part inside him that is crying out for just one drink of love.

Herbalife might put a spark in his eyes and some fat on his skinny bones, but it wouldn't deafen his ears to abusive language, and it wouldn't stop him from trying to please his demanding caretaker. He'd keep trying to do his auntie's bidding even though it made him cry until his mouth started bleeding.

That's the image I just can't shake from my memory. When I close my eyes, I can still see it. It haunts me tonight and makes me cry. An image like that changes a person forever.

The absence of the essential element of love is not just a condition of West Africa. It is missing all over the world. The absence of love is actually the absence of Jesus and redemption through Him. It is only through Jesus that we can bring real love to those who are missing it—because He is the only source of perfect love.

In this was manifested the love of God toward us, because that God sent his only begotten Son into the world, that we might live through him. Herein is love, not that we loved God, but that he loved us, and sent his Son to be the propitiation for our sins. . . . There is no fear in love; but perfect love casteth out fear: because fear hath torment. He that feareth is not made perfect in love.
—1 JOHN 4:9, 10, 18

CHAPTER SIX
MEMORIES OF TERROR

Note to parents: Please guide your children through this story; it contains graphic reality.

SOMETIMES I ALMOST forget that only eight years ago Liberia was in the midst of an awful, bloody, tribal civil war that left 200,000 people dead and threw this tiny West African country into world headlines. The war still causes terror in the hearts of those who went through it—because they will always remember.

Last Friday, I remembered as well.

I and several of the other expats, Elvin, Joe, and Marcus went to visit two schools. We went to distribute food parcels, take photos, interview guardians, and profile new children for CAM's orphan program. This aspect of our orphan program, called the "church orphan program," works through a pastor of a church and concentrates on vulnerable children living with guardians. Many of these children have lost one or both of their parents, or were abandoned. Our orphan program helps by supplying them with food each month, paying for their schooling and medical costs, distributing clothing, and making sure the children are living with married guardians and attending church.

As I said, sometimes it's easy to forget that this country experienced a war, because when we do the distributions at schools, everything seems so "normal," at least by West African standards. The children are so proud of their school uniforms; they love their colors. At one school, I noticed that even the bamboo flagpole was color-coded with painted rings of their school colors. We sat on rickety chairs and noticed the pieced metal roof with holes, the crooked sticks for rafters, the crumbling block gable, and the lizards scurrying on the walls. Yes, this was a typical Liberian school.

As Elvin and Joe interviewed guardians, Marcus took pictures.

Matthew Luogon and Sam Kparr, our Orphan Sponsorship Program administrators, had devotions with the guardians as I scribbled in my notebook and talked to the children, looking at their copybooks or listening to the interviews. But in the midst of West African normality, Hannah's story, as we say in Liberia, "grabbed me."

Hannah Gbatahlee and her brothers, Joshua and Ebenezer, sat in front of us in the little schoolroom. Their uncle told us their story—how they came to be eligible for the orphan program.

When the war intensified, I was hiding in the bush—but my brother, he was in the village when the Mandingos came. And since he was a young man, right away they just thought he was a Charles Taylor man (a soldier for the leader who had attacked the Mandingos). So they wanted to kill him.

The people begged for him, but to no avail. The soldiers, they just butcher him—they cut him into pieces. Then they take the pieces and put it in a wheelbarrow, and begin to sell it for 50 LD a piece. They killed him just like a goat, and then they forced the people to buy the pieces.

This man that they killed, he was my brother. And he was Hannah, Joshua, and Ebenezer's father.

As for me, I was hiding in the bush when this happened. Otherwise, the Mandingos would have killed me too. They killed six in my family.

But this is the children's story. Their ma, it is unknown where she is now. And for Hannah, she didn't even know the story until the other day, and Joe had to tell her "na mind" because she started crying.

And that is the terror we went through.

He said that last phrase with a sense of finality and moving on, as though it was time to put it behind us and go for lunch and keep on living. "That is the terror we went through."

But those three children sitting across from me on the bench in that little classroom—you can't tell me it didn't affect them. The story of terror impacted them, especially Hannah. She had this look in her eyes—I can't really describe it. How do you describe the look in the eyes of a child who just heard that her father was literally cut into pieces? Like her uncle said, she had started crying when she heard the story earlier in the week during the initial interview for the orphan program. And Joe had to tell her "na mind," which in this context meant, "It will be okay. It's all right now; you are safe."

Many of the orphans in Liberia don't know their whole story—or the true story. The adults in their lives hide it from them. But not talking about it doesn't take it away. The secrets will be revealed someday, and the children will discover how their moms or dads died.

When we left the school, it was still typical West Africa. Little children were playing with their homemade toys or "licking dust" (snacking on some after-school sugar candy). A crazy woman was walking about the churchyard, yelling absurd things. As we inched through a traffic jam on the way home, Elvin considered buying a huge fish at the bridge. I noticed political slogans all over the place because of the upcoming elections, along with headlines such as *Ma Ellen Begs for Votes*.

MEMORIES OF TERROR | 31

This is typical, and I don't feel the terror of war right now.

But the door is not so easily closed on the terror these people went through. Young children are just discovering the awful truth of how their parents died. It is real to them, because the terror was real.

My hope is that when more orphans find out the true story, someone will be there to tell them it's all right to cry. Someone will be there to care for them. Someone will be there to tell them "na mind"—that they are loved, safe, and protected after the terror they went through.

I am hopeful for the church orphan program. Yes, it has its cons just like most things in life do. But I like to think of this quote from Bob Pierce, founder of World Vision: "Don't fail to do something just because you can't do everything."

Ideally, "everything" in this case would include a safe, loving Christian home for every one of the 750 orphans on our church program to get the love and care they need. I realize not all of their guardians are providing that, but some are.

Even though the schools in Liberia are less than ideal, they are better than no schools. Many of the students did not attend school at all before they were on the orphan program. Now every school-age child on the program is going to school.

We do what we can. God helps us with our efforts, and He does what we can't do. He can work miracles in hearts and lives that are suffering the terrible consequences of war. We do our part, and we pray to unlock the door to a brighter future for the children of Liberia.

For I know the thoughts that I think toward you, saith the LORD, thoughts of peace, and not of evil, to give you an expected end.
–JEREMIAH 29:11

32 | SOME KIND OF LOVE

CHAPTER SEVEN

TWO WEEKS AND ONE CAN

IN APRIL, BABY TEE came to our office with his grandmother, Boita Gbar. She lived in Gben Gbars Town and cared for Baby Tee, whose mother was at the Redemption Hospital, sick. Baby Tee was remarkably underdeveloped. He was about the size of a newborn, even though he was eight months old.

Boita was extremely grateful for the two cans of Isomil baby formula we gave her. We instructed her to feed Baby Tee with only purified or boiled water out of a *clean* bottle. We told her we wanted to see Baby Tee again so that we could observe his improvement.

Two weeks later we went on a hunt for a baby and a grandma. We went to Gben Gbars Town, and all we had was a name, a town, and the distinct memory of a malnourished

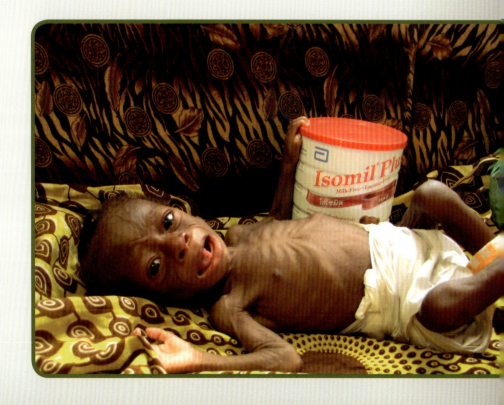

TWO WEEKS AND ONE CAN | 35

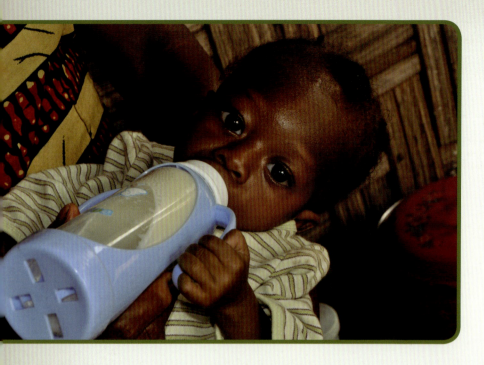

baby. He had been in such dire shape two weeks prior that we did not know if we would find him alive, thriving, or dead.

We followed one false lead after another until finally one girl said she knew who we were talking about, and she led us to Boita's hut. There we were thrilled to find Baby Tee looking ever so much better! What a miracle, seeing such marked improvement after only two weeks and one can of Isomil. Baby Tee had started gaining weight, and his ribs were no longer jutting out of his chest.

Boita began telling us more of her grandson's story. She said his mother had needed a Caesarean section when Baby Tee was born. She was a young mother, only twenty years old. After the surgery, she had complications and was in and out of Redemption Hospital. Sometimes she would even act crazy. Some people said it was an "African sign" (witchcraft), but Boita emphatically said it was not. They prayed earnestly for her, and she was healed of her mental illness.

We visited awhile longer with Boita and took pictures of Baby Tee. When we wanted to take off his shirt for an "after" picture, Baby Tee cried and cried. It seemed his clothes were his security. Marcus and Brother Dirkson encouraged Boita to feed Baby Tee some other food as well, like green plantain and bony fish, ground powder fine. These foods contain protein that would make the baby strong. But they told her to be careful because the baby's stomach was still small and tight and could not handle what a healthy eight-month-old child can.

Boita was so grateful for the milk. After her grandson drank a full bottle, she said, "His eyes are shiny! Thank you plenty!" She has a tough life, living in a little hut and caring for her grandchild. She said the baby's pa had deserted them: "Just left the baby ma and baby in my hand—sick and all."

Thankfully, Boita can now rest assured that Baby Tee is getting nutrition. And her faith in God, which caused her to say "no" to her daughter's witchcraft diagnosis and "yes" to prayer and faith in God, is enough to take her through the hard times of her life in Liberia, West Africa.

Her **faith in God** is enough to take her through the hard times of her life in Liberia, West Africa.

CHAPTER EIGHT
SIMPLE THANKSGIVING

THIS THANKSGIVING, I am thankful for my mom and dad. That may sound uncreative, like when you go around the circle naming what you're thankful for and everyone says things like clothes, food, and houses. But I guess I'll be simple this Thanksgiving season. I am thankful for my mom and dad because I was reminded recently of the enormity of what they've given me.

Prince's wound goes deep. Just yesterday he came to our office again. In September we were first introduced to Prince, and here's the story of what happened then.

In the afternoon, we left for Marca Medical Clinic in Monrovia—Marcus, me, three women, five babies, and one little boy. We all piled into CAM 101, our truck. Three baby mas (mothers with babies) sat in the back seat of the truck, two holding sets of twins. I sat in the front with the little boy, who was brother to one of the babies. With the exception of Marcus, who was driving, all of us held at least one child.

We got to Marca Clinic and sat down under a tree on benches and chairs. Prince had a twin named Princess, and they were four months old. Prince was extremely weak and tiny. He couldn't hold up his own head. In sharp contrast, Princess was as healthy as could be. For some reason, she accepted her mother's breast milk and Prince did not. At least that was the story told by Musu, their mother. But how can you tell? Was she really trying to treat them the same? She had been feeding Prince water out of a bottle. Had she even tried to give him any of her milk?

Marca, the nurse, checked the babies and provided them with CAM-donated meds—Omnicef, Daytime cold & flu syrup, Similac baby formula, and Isomil baby formula.

After being in Africa for a while, sometimes I don't notice the great differences between America and Africa anymore. But there were some things I couldn't help but notice that day.

When we get sick, we go to a sterilized, clean clinic and receive printed prescriptions. Then we go to sterile, clean pharmacies to get them filled. Here, the clinic office was dark and smelly. The waiting room was either outside or in a small carport-like area. The prescriptions were written on some sort of masking tape and affixed to the medicine bottles.

The differences are so vivid, yet for people who don't know the difference, maybe it doesn't matter. What does matter is that these little babies get the help they need to grow into healthy, strong children.

What mattered was that Prince was still alive and had received the milk he badly needed. I had faith that he could grow strong and healthy. Just seeing him drink that little bit of milk at the clinic gave me that reassurance. But I wondered if his mother cared enough about him to bother feeding him more than water. Would Prince get the milk we gave, or would his mother give it to his sister? Musu lived way out in the bush, a forty-five-minute canoe ride from the mission base—we couldn't go check up on her every day.

As I came face to face with great need, I thought of what Marca said after she saw the sad state of the children: "What to do? Where to start?"

I answered the question in my mind. We start by giving what's available—medicines and nutritional products. We start by praying for the babies and their health. We start by praying for change in Liberia, that the power of Satan would be broken and God's love would penetrate every sad, broken, sinful heart.

Now fast forward two and a half months. It's November, almost December. Just yesterday Prince's mother Musu brought her twins to Tower Hill. She needed more nutritional milk, but she seemed almost unable to communicate with us. Princess was still chubby and healthy, while Prince was still tiny and malnourished. I held Prince; at first he cried, but then he snuggled up to me and fell asleep in my arms. He felt as light as a small newborn, and he was seven months old.

Marcus gave Musu more nutritional drink and told her she *must* give it to Prince, not Princess. Prince needed it so badly! I just wanted to keep him, to give him the milk myself and watch him grow. But I had to give him back to Musu.

Then they left. Sometimes it is easy to wonder what good our efforts did. But it's a start, and we couldn't refuse to help.

Then I think of my family, of my home—of the stark difference between the way I grew up and the way Prince and countless others here in Africa are growing up. I feel so unworthy, but at the same time extremely blessed. How parents relate to their children impacts their lives hugely. My parents' love and teaching impacted me far more than anything else in my life.

I've learned so much since I came to Africa. One of the biggest things is the huge importance of a strong family. I plead with you—in Liberian terms, *I beg you!*—tell your mom and your dad you love them and are thankful for them. If you are a parent, tell your children you love them and are so glad God placed them in your family. Tell them today. Sometimes it's hard for us to put that sort of thing into words. We want our parents or our children just to know it by our actions. And we can know by actions. But I'll be honest and say that when I get an email from my dad with the words *I love you*, it does something special to me. I almost always start crying when I see an email from him because I can picture him pecking at the keyboard to write it. Knowing that it takes some effort for him to type it out makes it more meaningful to me.

At a recent orphanage directors' meeting here at the office, Elvin Stoltzfus, the Orphan Sponsorship Program director, was teaching on the importance of leading the orphans in the right way. He reminded us that the richest man in the world cannot take any of his riches to heaven. When he comes to the point of death, all those riches stay behind. But the orphan directors can take one thing, and that is the children. Likewise, parents can take only those for whom they've been responsible: their children. By leading and loving their children in the right way, they can guide them to trust in Jesus, who will give them an eternal home.

Thank you, Mom and Dad, for touching my life in an eternal way. May we all reach heaven and live there together.

SIMPLE THANKSGIVING | 41

CHAPTER NINE
HE WILL REDEEM THEM

REDEMPTION. IT'S WHAT the struggling children in Liberia are longing for. They need to be rescued and bought back from the chains of suffering they've endured.

As Prince, Princess, and their mother Musu continued coming to Tower Hill for milk, we could see hardly any change in Prince. His growth remained stunted. Once he was sick with malaria, so Marcus took him to a clinic for help.

It seemed Prince's mother did not care about him. She hardly communicated with us and wouldn't look us in the eye. I wonder if she was bewitched or mentally disabled. Every time Prince and his mother came, Marcus would tell her in very plain terms to take good care of Prince, but we wondered if it helped. His signs of improvement were so small.

We were able to help Prince a little with nutritional milk when he came to us, and he would eagerly suck on the bottle. I clearly remember the last time I held Prince. It was almost Christmastime. He snuggled right up to me and fell asleep in my arms. I did not want to give him back to his mother. I felt like a part of me was being ripped away when I handed him back.

We didn't hear from them for a long time. Then just today we found out that Prince died.

It shouldn't be a surprise, but still it is. Even though we see so many needy children and babies, Prince was special.

Elvin, the orphan program director, had shown Prince's picture and told his story at Christian Aid's open house. I honestly thought he would make it somehow, that surely the nutrition in the milk would kick in someday and Prince would grow to be a healthy child. I thought maybe the mother

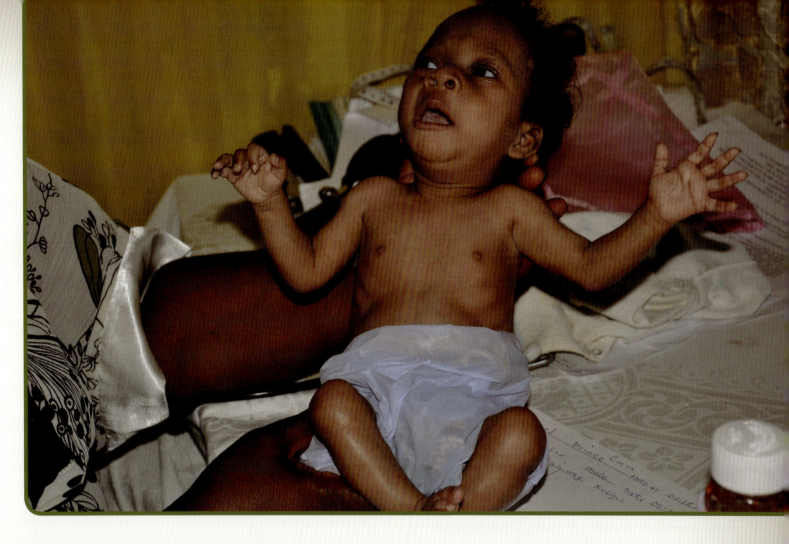

would wake up to the needs of her child, or maybe somebody else in the village would intervene.

Now I wonder how Prince took his last breath. I wonder if someone was holding him, or if he was just lying in *lapa* blankets in the corner of a mud hut somewhere. I wonder if it was in the nighttime, and no one knew he died until the next morning when they found his cold, little body stiff and silent. Or maybe it was in the heat of the day when he cried for the last time and took his final breath.

I wonder if Prince ever felt any love other than the times he came to Tower Hill, when we would hold him.

I don't like pat answers, the kind that say, "Prince is in a better place and it is all okay now." Even though I *know* he is in a better place, his death is still difficult. It shouldn't have happened the way it did.

But this reminds me of something my bossman said in his devotions

HE WILL REDEEM THEM | 43

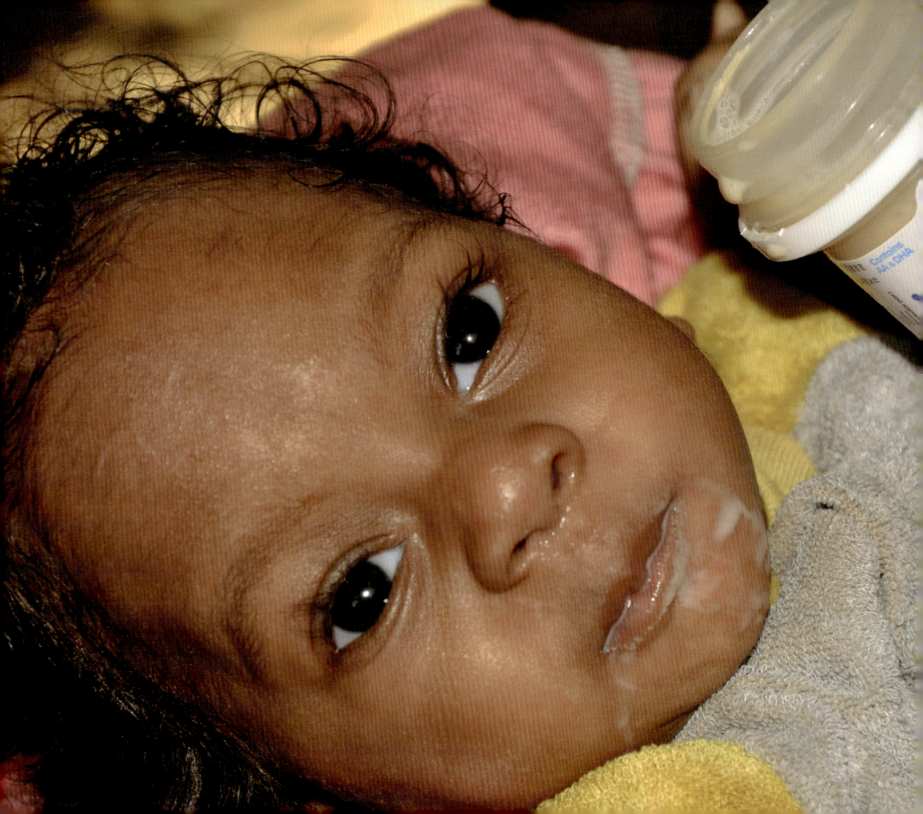

at prayer meeting the other Thursday evening. "God gives us too much to handle on our own so that we depend on Him." I think that is true. Sometimes God allows circumstances too big, too complex, and too tough for us to understand, so that we quit trying to figure it all out and simply believe in Him. I certainly can't figure out Prince's death. I don't see the reason for the brevity of Prince's life or why he had to die from neglect.

But I can choose to believe. I truly believe God's plan for Prince was perfected when this precious little boy breathed his last breath and went to heaven, where there's no sickness, pain, hunger, or death. I believe Prince is experiencing a kind of love that none of us have ever felt, a kind of love that will make all his suffering here on earth fade into oblivion.

I believe Prince is held in Jesus' arms, and no one will ever take him away.

I looked again at the pictures of Prince that were shown at the open house in November, and I was struck again with the implications of the verse at the end of the slideshow. I remember when Marcus found this verse during the many hours of working on pictures for the open house. This one just clicked—we knew Elvin would want to use it. We had no idea of Prince's future, but Jesus did redeem Prince from the oppression he had felt in his short lifetime.

He took Prince home to heaven.

He shall redeem their soul from deceit and violence:
and precious shall their blood be in his sight.
—PSALM 72:14

> He shall redeem their soul from deceit and violence: and **precious** shall their blood be in his sight.
> —PSALM 72:14

HE WILL REDEEM THEM | 45

CHAPTER TEN
PICTURES OF HOPE

I LOST MY heart to the children in Africa. This book is meant to tell their stories of hope, love, and redemption. Most of the stories happened right in my office or within five miles of where I lived, and most of them involved little babies who came for nutritional milk. Behind their eyes lay sad stories of lives God wants to redeem.

I write this book because every child's story matters. If no one feels their pain enough to write about it, few people would find out about them, and their stories would disappear into oblivion. Will this book change anything for them? It might not. Did it change me? Yes, it did. And I pray it changes you. When you see how God's love transcends everything to bring hope and redemption for starving, malnourished, and unloved children, you can never be the same.

JUNIOR KAKA

When Junior Kaka came to Tower Hill, his legs were too skinny for the rest of his body, and his eyes were huge circles in his little face. He was around two years old, but Comfort, his caretaker, didn't know his date of birth.

Holding a malnourished child brings an indescribable feeling. Not only is it obvious the child does not feel well physically, but most times you can see sadness in the big eyes—sadness from a life fraught with disease and abandonment. Junior had been abandoned by his mother. Rita Kaka deserted Junior and his two siblings and went to live in another town. Junior's siblings are living with his grandmother, and Junior lives with Comfort. Junior's father helps as he can, but he is busy with a new job.

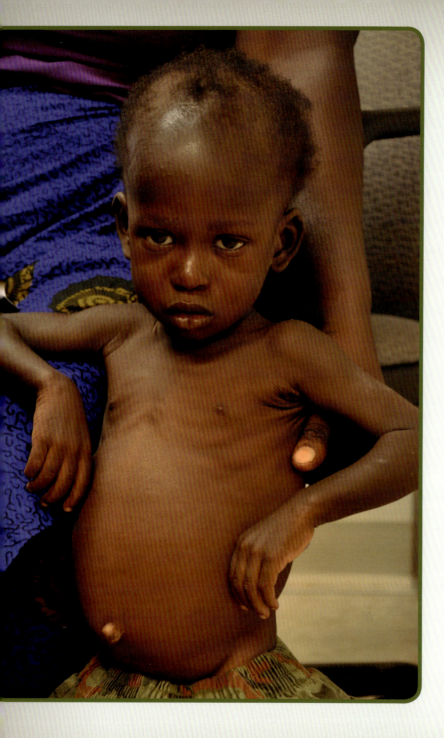

I wonder if Junior will ever see his mother again. Does Rita even care about her children? And if, at age twenty-four, she already has three children, does it even matter to her if she ever sees them again? I asked Comfort, "So Junior—his mother, she care if she ever see him again?"

Comfort answered, "No. No, she don't care."

We gave Comfort four boxes of nutritional drink for Junior, which will help him to grow strong physically. And we have hopes that Comfort will give Junior the love and care he needs, and that someday his big eyes will shine with security instead of being haunted by fear and pain.

VALENTINE MASSOQUOI

This little boy was born on February 14, 2011. His mother, Josephine Massoquoi, accordingly named him Valentine. Valentine was her third child, but during her pregnancy she did not go anywhere for checkups or eat a nutritious diet. And when little Valentine was born, he weighed a mere 2.2 pounds.

Josephine tried to feed him, but her milk was not enough for this little boy's body. His skin became pasty and thin, and every vein on his stomach was visible. Finally, in desperation, Josephine brought Valentine to Rock Clinic. Fatu, the nurse there, called us at Christian Aid Ministries and asked if we could please help. Through our medical program, we were able to provide Valentine with Isomil, donated by sponsors in America. Marcus showed Josephine how to prepare it, and we hoped to see good results in a little time.

One month later we went to see how Valentine was doing. We were so encouraged—he looked much better after only thirty days. Where his veins had previously been visible, a healthy layer of skin now covered them. We talked with the other ladies who lived in the household, and they told us the milk was helping.

"He getting fat and very happy-o!"

"I telling you, before, he could just be like a rat baby. He was so small!"

But now Valentine's eyes could focus, and he could even grasp a finger. The Isomil helped Valentine so much. Without its donation, he may not have survived.

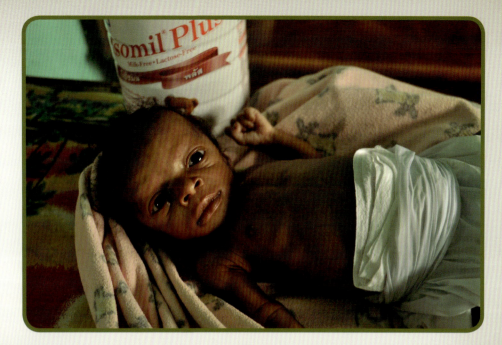

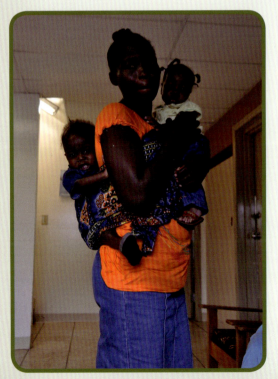

TRAVINA AND PERMILLA ZAZA

Kebeh Zaza, a thirty-eight-year-old lady from the village of Smell-No-Taste, came into our office with a sad story. In March of 2010, Kebeh's husband died from sickness. This left her with four children—and Kebeh was expecting twins.

Kebeh went to the C.H. Rennie Hospital in Kakata to have her babies. On July 17, she gave birth by Caesarean section to two girls, Travina and Permilla. The doctor failed to remove all of the surgical materials before closing Kebeh's incision, and it was left inside her stomach. Eventually, they transferred Kebeh to the JFK Hospital for another operation to remove the materials. There, the nurse did not give Kebeh all the pills prescribed to her, so her recovery was long. In all, Kebeh was hospitalized for more than five weeks.

When Kebeh left the hospital, she did not have any breast milk for her babies. Since she could not breast-feed them, she fed them water with a spoon. When

Kebeh brought Travina and Permilla to our office on October 29, they were so malnourished that their skin was wrinkled.

We gave them nutritional milk and were able to witness a miracle in just a few months. Travina and Permilla survived and grew into healthy little girls.

And I learned something. Love means a lot more than Valentine's Day gifts. The kind of love I learned in Africa is deeper. It's a heartfelt "thank you" from a beggar. It's the feeling you get when a little black finger wraps around your white one and then somehow wraps its way around your heart. It's watching the children play in the neighborhood soccer game. It's how you feel when you pull into an orphanage and twenty children come running out to meet you, crowding around your jeep before you can even open the door. It's knowing something about someone whose fingerprint is on your heart. It's the release of long-held bitterness. It's praying and knowing it's only God who can open the right doors at the right time. It's what happens when a baby cries until you snuggle him close, and he closes his eyes and falls asleep in your arms. It's laughing, making small talk, and bridging cultural barriers.

Love wears shoes every day, not just on Valentine's Day. We act it out when we become the hands and feet of Jesus, and we realize suddenly that it's only because of God's love and enabling power that we can work for Him. We don't have to try to love—it's something that Jesus just puts into our hearts.

> *If we love one another, God dwelleth in us,*
> *and his love is perfected in us.*
> —1 JOHN 4:12B

> **Love wears shoes** every day. We act it out when we become the hands and feet of Jesus, and we realize suddenly that it's only because of God's love and enabling power that we can work for Him.

SOME KIND OF LOVE

CHAPTER ELEVEN
NOT EVEN A SPARROW

TODAY WAS MY deadline crunch for an article about baby bundles and Kirk's vitamins for CAM's newsletter, and I had a huge stack of orphan profiles on my desk to process. While writing that article and entering all the orphan profiles into my computer for our sponsors in America, I got to thinking about life in Africa.

Life seems cheap here. But I get tired of hearing that and saying that, because it sounds like an excuse for not caring or for getting calloused to hard things in life. Maybe I am getting calloused. Well, all right—I know I am. Africa tends to do that to a person.

But God spoke to me through four little children today. He showed me life really isn't cheap, that every soul does have value. Here's how He showed me.

In my stack of orphan data, I processed a different kind of paper. Not a new orphan profile or orphanage transfer, but a notice—a death notice sent to a little girl's sponsor.

This orphan girl, Suah, had been so happy to receive a letter from her sponsor on Saturday, January 21. The administrator for her orphanage, Matthew Luogon, told me she was thrilled with the letter. She wanted to write a letter back, but she decided to wait until a little later because she thought she couldn't write well enough herself and wanted someone to help her.

But the very next day Suah suddenly got sick and her throat began to swell. The orphanage workers carried her by motorbike to a nearby hospital, but to no avail. Suah died that night.

We may never know the exact cause of her death. Healthcare in Africa is just like that. But I got to thinking—you know, Suah's

sponsor most likely wrote that letter weeks before it got to Liberia. It was first mailed to CAM's office in Ohio before it was personally delivered to Liberia and landed on my desk. Then I gave it to Elvin or Joe, who gave it to the Orphan Sponsorship Program administrator (Matthew) at their biweekly meeting, who took it on his motorbike to the orphanage, which is when he hand-delivered it to Suah. The delivery happened on a Saturday . . . the day before she died.

I really think God watched over that letter. And it got there on time—not a day too late.

Again, I tried to focus on the orphan profiles—eighty-seven of them. I was desperately trying to finish them before my deadline of 4:00 p.m., so after about the twentieth one, the stories all ran together and didn't make an impression on my calloused heart. Mother died in childbirth . . . father abandoned the child . . . mother was killed in an accident . . . father was poisoned . . .

Then number C16049 actually caused me to pause and swallow hard. "Found the child in a box on the dump pile. Guardian rescued him."

This two-year-old, Evant, was rejected by his mother and thrown in a box onto the junk pile. I wanted to gather the little fellow in my arms and hug him tight. I wonder if he knows what happened to him. If he doesn't know or comprehend it now, I

wonder how he will feel when he finds out he was rejected by his own flesh and blood—by the person who "born him," as we say in Liberia. Makes me think of the Liberian saying, "You can born the child, but not the heart." Just because you bear a child doesn't mean you can claim his heart—you have to love him too.

I hope someone loves him and that he can someday know in his heart that he is valued.

Because he is. All these children are.

My thoughts turned to tiny Patricia, who had come to our office with her auntie. Her thirty-six-year-old mother had thirteen children, and three of them died. Little Patricia was her last one. There were complications during the birth. Patricia's mother lived in Bahn, which is far from any good hospital. They took Patricia and her mother in an ambulance to the closest hospital, in Ganta. But it was too late—Patricia's mother hemorrhaged and died.

The family took baby Patricia and the body of her mother back to the village for burial. The village custom calls for all the women in the village to curse Patricia's mother for dying in childbirth, which they did for three days. During this time all the expectant mothers in the village left so that, according to their tradition, the curse of the childbirth death would not rest on them.

As for Patricia, no one loved her or cared much about her. She was passed from person to person until her auntie took pity on her and three of her siblings and began to care for them. Patricia desperately needed nutrients, so her auntie brought her to Monrovia and to our office for milk. She told us the poor little girl was so hungry that "every three hours, she can just want to eat!"

Thankfully, we have baby formula in our warehouse now and were able to give her Similac, which she loved and eagerly drank right up.

Again my mind was impressed with an image of another valuable soul. Kormassa Kollie brought her baby to us at Tower Hill on February 29, 2012. Her little baby's name is Godsgift, and she was only one and a half months old.

Godsgift was born with a cleft palate. The people in her village had never seen a baby with a cleft palate before, so they automatically assumed the baby was "witched." They said she had the evil spirit Gina, and the old ladies from the village told Kormassa she shouldn't feed the baby or give her a name—she should just let her die.

But Kormassa didn't. She came to town instead, all the way from her village, which was far away and cost her 1,005 LD, to find help for her tiny baby. She took her baby to Duside Hospital, and they gave her a special bottle to feed Godsgift, who had become malnourished. They also told her that she should bring the baby back the next year, when Godsgift would be old enough for an operation.

Kormassa told me her story.

"When my baby was born, she was just like this. For all of us, we never saw anything like it before. And the people of my village, they say the baby has Gina. All the ole ma's in the bush, that is what they told me. They told me not to feed it, not to even give it any

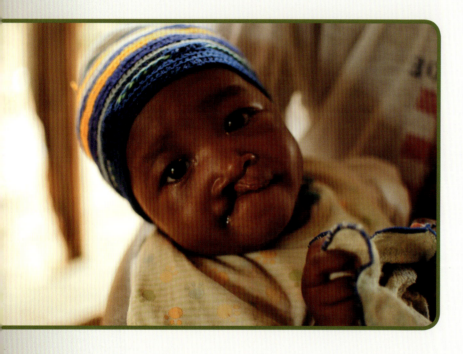

name. I called it Weedor, after my mother-in-law, but no way. My mother-in-law refused to have my baby named after her, so I called it something else. I called it Godsgift instead.

"I came all the way from Voinjama, Lofa County, to see if I couldn't find help for my baby. And my baby—oh, she was getting too dry (losing weight) because there was no way I could feed her, and I had no milk or bottle for her either.

"So I came here for help. I need milk for my baby. And I will stay here until the next year can reach. I will stay here where I can get help and food for my baby. And someday, by God's grace, maybe they can do operation on my baby and she can be healed. And I can go back to my village and they will see that it not Gina, it not any kind of spirit.

"Because she is my baby. My gift from God. That is why I called her Godsgift."

Thanks to our generous supporters, we were able to give Kormassa and her baby Similac infant formula. Kormassa and her husband and three of their children came and lived in town, in hopes of getting surgery done on Godsgift. They left their two-year-old toddler with a caretaker in Lofa County. The three children they brought with them went to school in Monrovia, and Godsgift was able to get in line for surgery when an American doctor came to offer services to underprivileged children at Duside Hospital.

In November, when Godsgift was ten months old, she underwent surgery at the hospital, and her cleft palate was repaired. Godsgift had a lot of pain as she healed from the surgery, and she refused to eat much. But while she cried, her mother smiled. Her little girl, her little Godsgift, had been healed.

Kormassa and her family returned to their village with Godsgift.

She was happily reunited with her daughter, now three years old, whom she hadn't seen for almost a whole year. And she took a special gift back to her village—proof of a miracle, not of Gina or a witch—a gift from God.

Despite the routine of eighty-seven orphan profiles, God showed me how much He values individuals. Suah, Evant, Patricia, and Godsgift—they are precious, and I thank God for giving me the chance to be here in Liberia and hear these stories and feel in my heart that life has value, no matter the circumstances.

Are not five sparrows sold for two farthings, and not one of them is forgotten before God? But even the very hairs of your head are all numbered. Fear not therefore: ye are of more value than many sparrows.
—LUKE 12:6-7

CHAPTER TWELVE
WHAT I LEARNED IN A WEST AFRICAN VILLAGE

Note to parents: Please guide your children through this story; it contains graphic reality.

BODA WEAH—A VILLAGE in Rivercess where poverty is a way of life. Ragged, half-clothed children and leaking thatched roofs are as common as the potholes and washouts of the long road leading to the village, dusty in dry season and muddy in rainy season.

Several of us workers from CAM went to Boda Weah for a day and a night. Joe needed to interview children for entry into the orphan program. He needed to make sure the children entering the program are in a home with good guardians and will receive the care they need. I went along to work on a feature story for CAM's open house.

We sat under the orange tree as Joe and Uncle Marvin Vah, the Orphan Sponsorship Program administrator for the area, interviewed the children. Marvin served as the interpreter, since the villagers' first language was Bassa and they couldn't speak English very well.

That is, except for one lady. When Joe asked her, "You getting me?" she answered, "No, I not getting you." We all laughed—she obviously understood him.

Anyway, the children came and perched in the woven wooden chair under the orange tree to be interviewed. While they waited and answered questions, once in a while they would dare to look me in the eyes.

They are just like other children. If you look them straight in the eye and smile, they will do exactly what other children do—look away from your eyes. But they can't quite hide the grin sneaking in at the corners of their mouths, no matter how hard they try.

I learned many things in this West African village.

I learned that time is remembered differently. When Joe was profiling the children, he would ask the guardian when the child was born, or the year the parent died. Oh, no idea, they would say. Finally Marvin explained to us that they remember things in terms of what happened. Such as, if there was an election a certain year, they will remember events that happened around that time, rather than the date of the events.

Units of measurement are the same way. Good luck getting a concrete figure if you ask someone how many acres of rice or cassava they are farming. They have absolutely no idea. But they have to have some unit of measurement. Finally Joe figured out how to measure farm size by the bucket. You know how big your farm is by how many buckets of seed rice you plant. For instance, Bobby, our contact person in Boda Weah, has a three-bucket rice farm.

I learned how school is vastly different in Boda Weah than in America, how it feels to have a Liberian lady plait your hair, how to suck oranges, and how to brush my teeth with a tiny bit of water in a bottle. I got pretty good at spitting toothpaste far into the bushes. Oh, I learned that rats in the ceiling at night evoke an uneasy feeling in would-be sleepers. And I learned the hard way that mosquitoes bite you like crazy if your legs get out from under the mosquito net during the night.

I learned how the ladies use the starchy root of the cassava plant to make farina, a type of flour. I also learned that if you are really hungry, you can even eat rice for breakfast.

But these little lessons fade when you learn about the stories of children.

I learned about a little boy called Chanchu Glapokpah. He's in our orphan program, and he's the little fellow we featured in "Liberia Through the Eyes of a Child" at one open house.

Chanchu's mother never loved him like most mothers love and care for their children. She abandoned him right after he was weaned, and she never came back to his village to see her little boy.

Some time later, Chanchu's father, Nyanyon, was eating a meal

after a funeral in the village. He refused to share his dish of food with another man—a deliberate, serious insult in Liberian culture. The man got so angry that he decided to poison Nyanyon. The two men may have had a history of offense, but we'll never know for sure. So Nyanyon was poisoned, and he died. For all practical purposes, this left Chanchu an orphan.

Sarah, Chanchu's aunt and guardian, told us Chanchu's story. She cried as she told us how Nyanyon was poisoned.

Poisoning is fairly common here in Liberia. Usually because of jealousy or anger, a person will take a certain poisonous plant and make a dust from the leaves. The dust is so poisonous that they just put it on their fingertips and touch the lip of a cup—and the person who drinks the liquid dies.

That's what happened to Chanchu's father. The person who poisoned him then had to leave the village of Boda Weah, or the other villagers probably would have killed him. And Chanchu is left to grow up without a family in Boda Weah.

Mecee and Kayatue are two other little girls Joe interviewed and added to CAM's orphan program. Their mom died the same way Chanchu's father did—she was poisoned.

Those are just three children's stories, and I heard many others. I learned that the spiritual darkness can weigh on your heart and soul until you can almost physically feel it.

I heard stories that still haunt me. Some still make me feel sick to my stomach. I learned that if a man wants to start a village, he needs to take a virgin, bury him or her alive, and plant a tree on top of the body. That's the start of his village. Supposedly that will cause it to prosper.

I heard how a few years ago the devil swallowed fifteen children. That is how they say it. It's how they describe children who die after going into the bush to join the Secret Society. Those within the society cut and mutilate the children, and many bleed to death or die from other complications. And so they say the devil swallowed them.

Imagine telling a mother that three of her children died this way—swallowed by the devil. It happened in Liberia, and their mother had to be told about it.

I learned how the government in power in Liberia today is exalting the devil more than God. Political parties will sacrifice humans—even their own children—to win an election. The people believe in these powers so much that sometimes they give whatever they think it will take to appease them, whether it is the eye of a human, an ear, or a heart.

Marvin told me these stories, and I will never forget the feeling I got afterward. Standing in that village between our vehicle and Bobby's mud hut, I knew he wasn't just telling me scary African stories. This was real, and I could feel it weighing on me to the very core of my being.

The spiritual darkness in Africa sometimes sinks into my soul, and I get this helpless feeling, this feeling that it's impossible to spread Jesus' light here because it will just be overpowered by Satan.

It is an awful feeling, that helplessness. But it doesn't last too long, because I know there is a Power beyond what I feel at the moment. So often I know it in my head but can't always feel it in my heart.

But I can feel it tonight. I am at home sitting outside on my concrete steps, feeling great except for all my mosquito bites. I'm all wrapped up in my brown and orange *lapa* blanket even though it is probably 75 degrees out here, but it feels good. I'm listening to the night sounds of Africa and looking at the stars. And I feel Jesus and His love in a deeper way than I did before. The only way I can explain it is that when you see certain aspects of the darkest side of human nature, then the alternative, the opposite, is so much brighter.

Tonight one star is way brighter than all the others. I think it must be a planet. That is how I imagine Jesus' love and power to be—because even though the black of night is so vast, that one "little" planet or star still hangs there, so bright and brave. I know that *brave* is not usually an adjective you use to describe a star. Still, I say this star is the bravest star I have ever seen. It reminds me that Jesus' power is real here in Africa, because even in the seemingly vast and infinite dark state of sin, there is always, *always,* at least a pinprick of light.

I wish I could end with a miraculous story and say that Jesus came to this African village and the spiritual darkness is gone forever. That the little boy called Chanchu and the little girls, Mecee and Kayatue, will choose to follow Jesus and will always have someone to love and care for them as they grow up. I wish I could say that will happen without a doubt.

I wish I could. But I can't say that yet.

Still, I believe there are people in the village who believe in Jesus and are doing what is right. As best as they know how, they are living a godly life.

And I believe that even in the midst of deep spiritual darkness, the power of Jesus is real, and this power is available for us to claim in our lives.

Please pray with me that Satan's power would be "blasted apart," as we say in Africa, and that Jesus' love would penetrate every dark, sinful village and heart.

To open their eyes, and to turn them from darkness to light, and from the power of Satan unto God.
—ACTS 26:18A

> Jesus' power is real here in Africa, because even in the seemingly vast and infinite dark state of sin, there is always, always, at least a **pinprick of light.**

CHAPTER THIRTEEN
TWO BABIES AND THE BREATH OF LIFE

TWO BABIES, ONE in America and one in Africa. One with white skin and one with black. One with loving parents, the other with a mom and dad who aren't married and live in abject poverty.

So different, but both fighting, struggling for life and breath.

Hazaiah Martin is the grandson of my fellow missionaries, Jerry and Rhoda Martin. He was born with the chromosome disorder Trisomy 13.

Some Trisomy 13 babies die while still in the womb. Some live a few hours, days, or weeks, and in extremely rare cases, some live for several years. The three main symptoms of Trisomy 13 are facial clefting, extra fingers, and heart problems. If a Trisomy 13 baby has no other life-threatening problems, he will eventually die when the brain stops telling him to breathe.

Hazaiah was born on October 1, 2011, seven weeks early. He weighed 3 pounds, 3 ounces. His name means *God will decide*.

He received top-notch care at the hospital and was showered with love and prayers and songs from his parents and family. In Africa, Jerry and Rhoda continued their work, waiting to hear news from home and their grandchild, but feeling so far away. Rhoda forwarded me his updates because I wanted to find out how Hazaiah was doing.

And now the other little baby . . .

T-Boy lives only a few miles away from us, in Scheiffelin Town. He is awfully malnourished, tiny, and sick. As a last resort, his mother, Mamie Glaybou, brought him to our office asking for help. She sat beside me and told me the story of her baby.

T-Boy weighed only 14.5 pounds at nine months old. His paper-thin skin hung over his fragile bones. I pulled off his sock to look at his foot, and I was afraid that his foot or at least some of the thin skin on his leg would come off along with the sock. That is how weak and frail his body looked.

> Life is a miracle, and God holds it in His hands.

Mamie said she took him to a hospital and a clinic, and they told her he has a sore in his stomach. What that is, I don't know, but the hospitals and clinics here are vastly different from the ones in North America. Obviously they weren't doing very much to help this little boy.

That was last Thursday, October 20. We gave T-Boy Herbalife nutritional drink here at our office, and Marcus took him to a nearby clinic. There he received injections of ampicillin, gentamicin, and artemether for his severe bacterial infection and malaria. And as far as I know, T-Boy still survives today, fighting against the odds—for life.

But that same Thursday when T-Boy got a chance for health and life, Jerry and Rhoda bought tickets to go home. Their grandson, Hazaiah, had taken his last breath in the arms of his loving mother.

Two boys, two lives—so vastly different, but each was given the breath of life by a loving God. Culture, time, and poverty have no real power over that breath; God chooses when to give it and when to take it away.

I can't help but think of three weeks ago when Pa Jerry had the topic at Wednesday night prayer meeting at Hope Mennonite Church—just a dimly lit shack with wooden benches, a swept concrete floor, pallet walls covered with black fabric of some sort, and the ever-present lizards running on the ceiling.

As Pa Jerry spoke, he knew that his little grandson Hazaiah was struggling to survive. His subject that night was "Jesus, the Great Physician." He said we are not able, but God is able; that we don't have control over life, but God does; and that there is no sickness, no bondage, no problem so great that Christ, the Great Physician, cannot heal. "Without Jesus we can't face anything. But with Jesus we can face everything." Pa Jerry, whose own heart must have been nearly breaking, said this.

Then he prayed, and I remember so clearly what he said: "God, life is a miracle, and you hold it in your hands." God is able—more than able. He is the Creator of life and breath, and each child's breath is created and directed by God.

Each one of Hazaiah's breaths was given to him by God.

And each one of T-Boy's is too.

I believe that little Hazaiah's short stay on earth glorified God, maybe even in ways it never would have had he lived longer. God is glorified through life—and death. I believe that both of these babies show us that life on earth, however long or short, is worth living for God's glory.

CHAPTER FOURTEEN
TELL THE TRUTH

WE BOUNCE ALONG to Peace Island. At the entrance, heaps of awful-smelling garbage line the rocky, rutted road. Young children who should be in school are digging around in the filth, finding small pieces of wood to carry home in plastic bags. Their families cannot afford to buy charcoal to kindle their fires and cook their rice. Digging through garbage is the solution of choice. We drive past the market, where women sell little piles of bitterball, onions, peppers, and chicken cube (bouillon), as well as bigger piles of bush meat (any creature found in the bush), chicken and pig feet, and dried fish. We drive past a soccer field, where boys kick a tattered ball around.

Peace Island is a rocky island rising out of the Monrovia swamp. It is surrounded by mangroves in all directions. Before Liberia's civil war, Peace Island was just a piece of land near Monrovia, Liberia's capital city. Few people lived there; it was just bush and farmland. It was designated to become housing for the military officers or soldiers during Samuel Doe's regime. But during the war, it became a refugee camp; since the war, it has become a temporary community. I say "temporary" because there are rumors that everyone will need to leave the island because the government wishes to reclaim the land.

We come to Elisha's house. Smoke from a low fire to dry fish wafts up from pieces of tin over the fire and fills my nostrils. An old lady halfway listens to our conversation while sweeping the ground with a country broom. We sit on tiny benches. Baby Elisha cries, and we take him to his caretaker and she feeds him. He soon falls asleep, full and happy once more, oblivious to the world he inhabits.

Elisha's parents, Peter and Princess, had five children before Elisha was born. Peter met Princess during the war. He is a Kpelle man from Bong County, but the war forced him to flee to Grand Bassa County, where he met Princess in the Number 2 District.

Eventually they moved to Monrovia and made their home in a makeshift shelter on Peace Island.

Princess discovered she was expecting again, and throughout her pregnancy she would complain of stomach pain. She went back to visit her home in Grand Bassa County, Number 2 District, but came back the end of August.

On August 28, Princess went to the midwife, but she sent Princess home, saying, "That just slow pain!" Peter told Princess to go back to the midwife again, so she took her sister along and went.

A few days later Elisha was born. Something was wrong, however. The midwife was confused, because there were two cords but only one baby—and signs of infection. Something was amiss.

Then Princess confessed. She'd had an abortion. And it was successful—at least, partially. It killed one baby. But what they didn't know was that there were two babies inside her womb. Princess had been expecting twins.

One baby had been killed, but little Elisha still had the precious breath of life.

Elisha was alive but injured. His eyes did not focus well and seemed to be glazed over, maybe even indicating blindness. But he was alive.

Princess, though, struggled to survive. Her body was not able to handle all that had transpired, and as Liberians say, she kept "falling off," which means she could not talk and was unconscious.

Elisha had been born at the midwife's house on Friday. The next

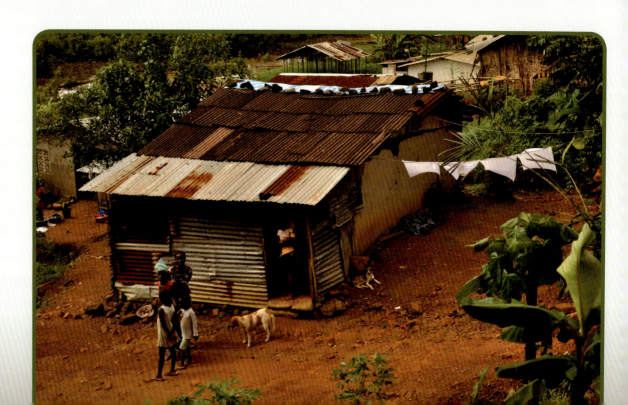

70 | SOME KIND OF LOVE

day, Saturday, the midwife called Peter and told him Princess was not doing well. Peter went to the midwife's house and took Princess to Benson Hospital by taxi car. The hospital staff admitted her and gave her "drip," the Liberian term for IV.

Baby Elisha stayed with the midwife.

But Princess' condition worsened. They transferred her to another hospital and put her on oxygen. Peter came to be with Princess and stayed until 8:00 that evening, but she was unresponsive.

On Sunday morning Peter received a call from the hospital. The person on the phone told him he must come to the hospital. Peter heard someone in the background saying, "Why can't you tell the man the truth?"

So they did. They told him the truth—his wife had died.

Princess was buried on September 6. Her parents came from the interior for the burial, and they took three of the children back with them to stay. Peter stayed on Peace Island in his partially finished house. He hired someone to take care of newborn Elisha, but he needed milk.

David and Esther Nuon are neighbors to Peter, and David works at Christian Aid Ministries. He asked Marcus for milk, and that is how little Elisha survived those first few days.

But the story is not over.

Soon after Princess died, her best friend, Julie, went into labor and gave birth. But her baby died. Julie wanted to do something for her friend, so she took little Elisha into her own home and breast-fed him. She is now caring for this little boy and doing all she can for the one who, in the world's eyes, was not supposed to live.

But the truth is, Elisha survived—and I can tell his story. The words the hospital staff told Peter keep ringing in my ears: "Tell the man the truth."

Something burns inside me because now I know and feel the truth. I researched the conditions of this country. It is true—1 in 24 women die in childbirth,[1] and 1 in 9 children die before their fifth birthday.[2] This means that an average of 32 children die in this tiny country (the size of the state of Tennessee) every single day.

I used to read statistics like this and think about them briefly, but now I feel them deeply. Today, on one side of me sat a man with no wife, and on the other side of me sat a mother who carried her baby for nine months, lost it, and is now feeding another's. And that baby's twin was forced to die.

It is no longer just a United Nations researched statistic. It is life in Liberia, and it is truth.

---

[1] "Child Info: Monitoring the Situation of Children and Women," June 2012, <http://www.childinfo.org/maternal_mortality_indicators.php>, accessed on February 14, 2013.

[2] *The Situation of Children and Women in Liberia: From Conflict to Peace* (UNICEF), 2012, p. 4.

Freedom comes from knowing the truth. The horror of sin and disease in this sin-cursed earth is only part of the truth; the other part is that the truth of Jesus' redemption makes it possible for us to deal with this sin-cursed world.

When we grasp Jesus' redemptive truth, we become free to live fully and help others. Now that I know children like Elisha, I care more deeply. I now understand what Jesus meant when He said, "Know the truth, and the truth shall make you free." After all, the dusty paths I walk on in Liberia are not unlike the dusty paths Jesus walked on when He was helping, healing, and teaching the lost of the world.

The truth of Jesus now helps me to live a life that fights the odds to change the world, one small child at a time. His truth gives me freedom to bring hope to the hopeless and light to those who walk in darkness.

And ye shall know the truth, and the truth shall make you free.
—JOHN 8:32

> Freedom comes from knowing the truth. And when we grasp Jesus' redemptive truth, we become **free to live fully and help others.**

CHAPTER FIFTEEN
REBECCA'S GIFTS

I ALWAYS KNEW God was real and that He had the power to perform miracles. I knew it in my head, but it wasn't until I saw a miracle with my own eyes that I felt I could reach out and touch that wonder-working Hand.

Right in front of my eyes, I saw a living miracle. I saw how God works in ways far beyond anything we can think or even imagine. And His ways are anything but predictable.

It was as real as the red dirt beneath my feet. As real as the mornings in the village of Garplay—the conversations in Gio, the scratching of brooms on the hard-packed earth, the clatter of cook pots, and the chattering of toucans in palm trees.

That's how present God is. That's how real He is to Rebecca and her babies.

Rebecca is a widow whose husband was killed in an automobile accident. She lives in the village of Garplay, on the grounds of a mission. Established by Americans before Liberia's civil war, the mission now includes a church, school, and clinic run solely by the Liberian people. Rebecca gives vaccinations to people at the clinic. She earns only 80 USD per month from her job and uses all that money to raise her eighteen children. Oh, they're not all her biological children. Many of the babies' mothers died in childbirth; some have no parents at all. But now they are no longer motherless—they are *her* children. Here is her story, in true Liberian English.

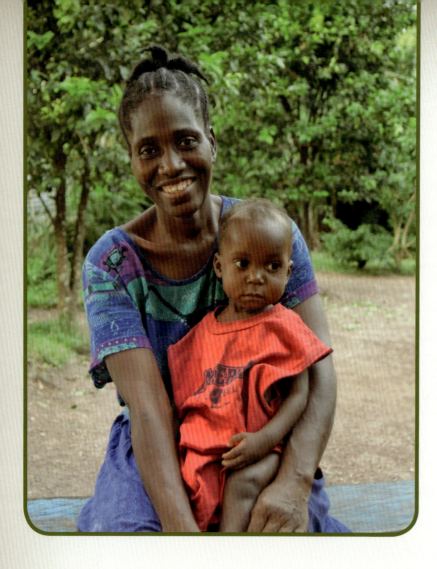

I was living there at the mission, after my husband died in 1997. I lived at the mission with my four children and worked in the clinic as the vaccinator.

I could always be seeing malnourished children, and I was the vaccinator for surrounding villages; so I travel with my bag of vaccinations to surrounding villages, to vaccinate children, babies, and mothers—vaccinate them for things like polio, tetanus, and diphtheria.

The first girl I took in was Delu. Her name was *whose child is this*. I saw that when she was in her home, every time I would see her, she would be looking very bad. So I took her into my own home to save her life. I fed her benne seed (sesame seed), plantain, and bony fish. And the little girl did very well. And that was just the beginning of my ministry, of taking in babies whose mothers had died and the babies were becoming malnourished. Soon people started bringing babies to me, babies whose mothers died in childbirth. The babies needed help and good food to survive. And I did it because God gave me this job, and without me taking care of these babies, I knew they would suffer so much and maybe even die.

So I was here on the mission working at the clinic and taking care of babies in my tiny house, when I started to experience so much pain. I had a sharp pain in my stomach—like an object or something was in there. And so I suffered, all through 2004, 2005, and 2006. I told the clinic staff about it, and they were praying with me. Every Monday they would pray with me.

So we were there, praying. I didn't know what to do, because if I would leave for surgery, I would have no one to watch my babies for me. And I said, "God, if you want me to do this thing with the

76 | SOME KIND OF LOVE

children, then you the one who need to help me. I can't do it alone. I can't do it. I can't take care of all these little children without you."

So one morning, I got up at my usual time. I can always get up at about 5:30 to make soft rice for the children. I start the fire; then I go in and read my Bible. But that morning, something was different. When I went in, I fell into a heavy sleep. And I had a vision.

Two huge men, dressed all in white, came up to me. And the first one said, "Rebecca, Rebecca."

And for myself, I didn't even know what to say. So I said nothing.

Then he said they will perform surgery for me. And then it was like I could see myself in an operating room somewhere. They were operating on my own body, and I could see myself below on the earth. They did the surgery; then the other one came up to me and said, "Here is the thing that was in you." But it was like a tumor with a piece of bone on it. I was so confused, because there was some bone with the tumor, and if you have bone with it, how can you live okay? But the man told me, "Look, it is like this. The bone was already affected by the tumor. So we removed it too. But it will not affect you, it will be all right."

And then I woke up, and I was so tired. But I went to the clinic, and I was just lying down, because I was so tired. I told the nurse there that I was not able to do it that day. And she said, "What, Rebecca, that the first time I ever hear you saying that thing! What happened to you?"

So I told the staff what happened, and after that there was no clinic business that day. We were just rejoicing and praising God all day, because God healed me. He really did.

But my troubles, they were not over. There were some people who were so sure I was doing the wrong thing by taking so many babies in, and they just could not understand.

And what could I say? Because it was really a hard thing that I was doing, but I knew God wanted me to do it, because He was the one supporting me. But there were hard times.

But I was praying and I said, "God, if you don't want me to do this job, I won't do it. I won't take care of all these babies if this is not the right thing to do." But God wanted me to do it, He really did. He showed me through another hard thing.

My late husband's sister died, so I went to Ganta for the burial.

And it was so hard on me that she died—she was not just my sister, she my friend, and she and her husband tried to help my ministry. She worked at the Ganta Methodist Hospital, and she would bake cookies and take them with her to the hospital to sell. With that money, they were going to help me. But then she passed on.

So as I was leaving to go to Ganta for the funeral, my children were just crying on me. I had a baby girl there at that time, and I left them with just one small can of milk. And I knew it was not much, but what could I do? It was all I had. And my children, they said, "Mama, you leaving us with just one can of milk? And no money?"

I said, "Yes, but I will be back very soon." But they were so sad to see me going, too sad.

So then I went for the burial. It was a Friday that I went. But it was there that my brother told me something. He said, "My wife, she could be selling cookies at the hospital, to make small money for you. So I will give you the money on Monday. I got it all locked in a cashbox and will give it to you."

I was so amazed. Money, for me? Then on Monday he gave me the money. It was 2,750 LD (about 40 USD) and I was so happy for it. I went to the market, and I bought

REBECCA'S GIFTS | 79

diapers, I bought powder, I bought milk—I just couldn't even believe it. I was so happy because God, He did it for me!

So I came back the long road from Ganta to Garplay. The motorbike put me down right in front of the house, and the children all came running out to meet me. "Mama, Mama" they were calling, "you got milk?"

"Milk?" I laughed. "Yes, I got milk. I got it. God, He the one who did it for me!"

And He continued to help me.

Somehow, this was not just a story to me. This was so real. She was a real woman living in a tiny hut in a small African bush village. I'll never forget Rebecca telling me about herself and her children. She has been given the gift of health, but of greater importance to her are her children.

When we left, she was waving to me with a baby in her arms, smiling as if she had the best in the world to smile about. And maybe she does have the best in the world. She has a God who has given her a purpose and is meeting her needs.

Rebecca also gave me a gift. I will never forget that night when we were sitting by the cook fire. She sat there telling her story with about three little children around her in the glowing evening light. Everything faded in comparison to the light in her eyes as she talked

REBECCA'S GIFTS | 81

about how God took care of her and her children. Her entire face lit up as she said, "I don't really know how it can be; I just know God is providing for me. And if He will do it for me, then how can I say no?"

That's the gift she gave me—the realization that if God says, "Yes, I will enable you to do it," I have no reason to say no to His calling.

He made a way for her—Rebecca and eighteen children in her tiny hut.

He will make a way for you too.

> Rebecca does have the best in the world. She has a God who has given her a purpose and is meeting her needs.

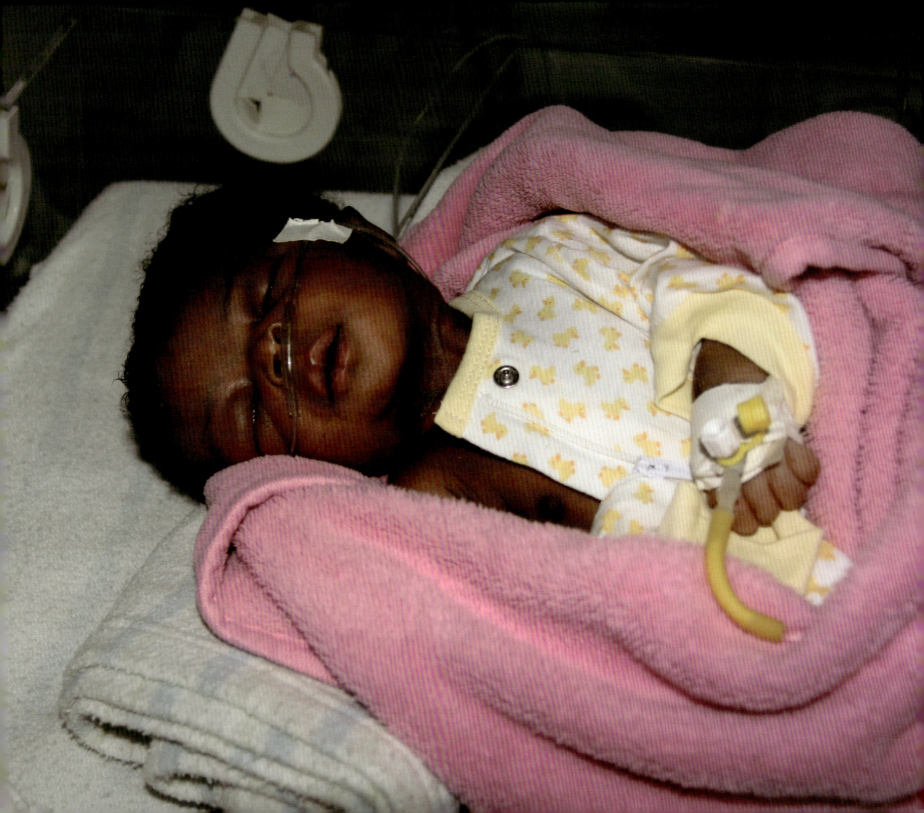

CHAPTER SIXTEEN

ONE KISS

TONIGHT I DON'T know how to explain my heart. I don't even know if what I'm writing is appropriate to print. But I am committed to writing about real life in Africa, so here it is.

It was Saturday afternoon. I was avoiding my office and greatly enjoying my day of sleeping in, sewing, cleaning, and steering clear of the work that had consumed all my waking hours for the past five days. Then Tracy stopped in the middle of her cleaning to tell me about her friend "who is catching a hard time at the hospital." I wasn't in the mood to listen to what seemed to be the thousandth story I've heard of sick people this rainy season, but I forced myself to listen. For some reason this story gripped me, so I said, "Let's go visit your friend."

When we got to the hospital, we were met by Tamba, a CAM employee. Tamba is a man with a heart the size of Africa and is a veteran of visiting people in Liberia's substandard hospitals. He helped us girls sweet-talk the security guards into letting us in before visiting hours. We then persuaded the nurses to let us see Tracy's friend's baby, because it was in a special ICU room of some sort. In this hospital, I discovered, you weren't allowed to bring food in for the patients. Too many patients had been poisoned by "friends" who turned out to be enemies. This *is* Africa. Still, we were able to sneak in some chicken noodle soup for her. I sat down with the baby ma (baby's mother) on the hospital bed, and she ate the chicken noodle soup we brought for her as she told us her story—every gory detail.

The pain grabbed her Monday night, and she knew she would have her baby soon. She was not married; she only had a boyfriend. This boyfriend had claimed he had no other children—which was a big lie. He was a married man with five children and now wanted nothing to do with his girlfriend's baby.

She went to a clinic on Tuesday morning. Since the woman in charge of the clinic wasn't there, another lady who was still in training tried to deliver the baby. But the baby didn't come for a long time. The woman in labor wanted badly to leave and go to a hospital, but the "midwife" didn't let her. Instead, she did a lot of damage to the baby, trying in vain to deliver it. Finally, on Wednesday night, after about thirty-six hours of labor, she released the baby ma to go to Benson Hospital.

At the hospital they examined her briefly and told her the baby was dead. They sent her on to JFK Hospital to deliver her dead baby, because at Benson they accept new patients by referral only. So this woman who had been in labor for more than thirty-six hours was taken in a rickety, bumpy taxi car to JFK. By then she was screaming from the extreme pain.

She finally gave birth to a baby girl on Thursday at noon at the JFK Hospital, almost three days after the pain first grabbed her.

But her baby girl didn't cry. She didn't even open her eyes. Her head was terribly misshapen, her eyes were swollen, and her jaw was mashed because of how the midwife had tried to speed up the delivery. Incredibly, though, she was alive and breathing.

This innocent child had an extremely traumatic arrival in this world, and she was struggling to live. It was all so unnecessary. Had it not been for the midwife's actions, she would likely have been a perfectly normal child.

I had never before seen such a misshapen head; it was stretched out of proportion. I didn't know baby's heads were so pliable when they are born. She was injured beyond help and couldn't even breathe on her own. Oxygen and feeding tubes were keeping her alive.

Tracy told us the baby ma said that the hospital was too expensive and the father couldn't afford to let her stay and continue her treatment. She said the doctor planned to give the baby an injection so that she would die. Then the baby would be taken to the morgue and hauled off or thrown into the garbage somewhere.

It sounds unbelievable, but believe me, it's the truth. Things like this happen here.

Tracy encouraged the mother to stay with her baby. So she is staying right beside her baby now. And as far as I know, the potential injection is just a story. But it is not an impossibility.

I don't see how the baby can survive. If I find out tomorrow there's just an empty bed with no baby in it, I'll easily believe it.

I could rant and rave at Liberian healthcare. How can you just throw a baby in the trashcan or give it an injection so that it dies?

I get so frustrated with the immorality and loose living of this country. When we were visiting at the hospital, the boyfriend came to see her. Before he walked into the room, she had been crying on us and saying, "He doesn't care about me or the baby." But when he walked into the room, her eyes totally lit up. I knew she still felt something for him. So who's to say the whole story won't just happen again? The whole thing made me feel like raging about life in general—it's so unfair.

But I've learned ranting and raving doesn't help. It just wastes my breath.

Tonight, I have more questions than answers, more realism than idealism . . . and more hurt inside my heart than anything else.

When you kiss an innocent baby's cheek and touch its little chest where the heart is trying so hard to beat, you can't help but feel the brevity and unfairness of life to the very core of your being. Your perspective on life changes direction completely.

And you know for certain that there is absolutely nothing in your power that can fix the hurt. Money cannot heal the ache or teach a mother to love her child. Better healthcare and higher education can help, but they don't solve the problem. There is only one cure to this sin-cursed earth—the redemptive love of Jesus.

After so many times, you would think I would get used to it. But I just don't.

You would think I could close my eyes and clench my teeth and forget about it and go on smiling and laughing. But I just can't.

You'd think I could go on with life and be the same person I was before. But I'm not.

My little girl died last night. Jesus took her home to heaven.

I don't think I'll ever get used to it. What makes it so sad is that it was a totally preventable and unnecessary way to live and die. I know she's better off in heaven, but it still seems unfair that her week here on earth was filled with pain and suffering.

She died without a name or a loving family. She never left the hospital where she was born, probably never even left the maternity ward. Her father disowned her, and her mother was helpless to

ONE KISS | 87

provide for her. Her nurses seemed to care little about her. She experienced tubes and a hospital bed instead of milk and soft blankets and a bassinet.

My little nameless girl whom I kissed one time. But she left a mark on my life and an ache in my heart.

> *Take heed that ye despise not one of these little ones; for I say unto you, that in heaven their angels do always behold the face of my Father which is in heaven.*
> —MATTHEW 18:10

> **Money cannot heal the ache or teach a mother to love her child. Better healthcare and higher education can help, but they don't solve the problem. There is only one cure to this sin-cursed earth—the redemptive love of Jesus.**

To the little baby girl with no name—

The only time I saw you was when you were fighting to live on that little bed in the hospital. I touched your little chest and I felt you breathing so hard.

And you mattered. Of course you matter to God, but you matter so much to ME too, because each life is precious. Like Jesus said, not one sparrow will fall from the sky without Him seeing it. That means that not one baby will die either without our Jesus seeing it. Even if they throw your body in the trash can, He'll pick you up and take you to heaven. Maybe you are in His arms already tonight.

I cry because it's not fair. Your brief stay on earth wasn't fair. You will be happier in heaven and will never want to come back, but every beat of your heart mattered.

I'm not sure if anyone ever held you on earth or if you ever snuggled up to anyone's chest and felt warm and loved. Maybe you knew only the little walls of your bed. But I saw you breathing, I felt your skin, and I leaned in and kissed you one time before I left, even though the nurses frowned at me. I did it because your life is precious, and you mattered to me. I loved you from the moment I saw you, and I haven't stopped praying for you.

Your short stay in Africa was not in vain. In some ways I am happy that just soon you will be in Jesus' arms and not on this sin-cursed earth. But I cry because I love you and it hurts to lose someone you love.

I love you, baby girl. I know you're safe with Jesus.

—Gloria

88 | SOME KIND OF LOVE

CHAPTER SEVENTEEN
INSIDE THE BAMBOO WALLS

MY NAME IS Martha, and I am the directress of Jesus Christ Children's Ministry. I will tell you my story.

Before the war, I worked with Christian Girls' Hostel. A woman who had gone to America and become a Christian was running it. We helped girls who were orphaned or abandoned.

But then the war came to Liberia. In 1992 I fled Liberia and went to Guinea for safety. I was just looking for somewhere, anywhere to go for safety.

Guinea is where I met my husband; he was working there with the UN. After some time we fled on to Danane, Ivory Coast. And that is where it all began. I began taking in girls who were orphaned or abandoned due to the war. And so began Jesus Christ Children's Ministry.

My husband said it would be easier to raise these children back home, so I came back to Liberia with some of the children. My husband followed with the rest of the children a month later.

So there we were—my husband and myself, with nine children. And 50 USD. It was God who helped us in those difficult times. We cut sticks from the bush to make a house for ourselves, and we bought some concrete to plaster the floors.

Then one day nine girls came from Cotton Tree. They needed help; the war disbanded all the families there and many were killed.

Back then, we lived one day at a time. We would pray, "Give us this day our daily bread," and we meant it. It was the only way we were able to survive.

Then in 2000 my husband got very sick. The doctors could do nothing for him, and he died. I didn't know what to do. I took some time away to mourn, but I promised the children and my helpers that I would come back. And I did—after three months, I came back to my home, back to my children. And I kept taking care of the children without him.

I had my big bunch of children during the war. The factions were just fighting, fighting, fighting. We could hear the gunshots from across the river. I gathered all my children in my room. Then we were afraid that was not safe enough, so we all huddled in the storeroom.

At that time I had twenty-nine children with me, and we were huddled together in that small storeroom. David, my nephew, came

and told me we need to get out, so we all gathered the children and ran down the road. I had a kerosene lamp and they told me to cut it, because we were so afraid the soldiers would see the light and begin to shoot.

We hid in the bush with all the little children, and finally we walked all the way to the next town. The next day we went back to get mattresses and food and our medicines. We were watching all the time for rebels, and we were so afraid. But we made it safely. After that we went up to the Church of God and lived in there for three weeks. We ate corn seeds for breakfast.

Then I decided to come back to White Plains, but by then the rebels were all over the place, and it was more dangerous, and we were running out of food. One day, we just had no food. I had 800 LD, so I went to Red Light to find food for my children.

While I was gone, a rebel came and asked for one of my girls. He demanded to take my oldest one; she was fourteen years old. David, my nephew who was in charge while I was gone, refused to give her. He stood his ground, even when the rebel soldier said, "Look, my own name is next to God. Give her to me." And he even fired his gun in the air. But David refused to give her.

The rebel soldier finally gave up and left, but he said he is coming back the next day for the girl.

So when I came back from Red Light and heard the story, I said, "Okay, I will take my girls away. I will take my girls to somewhere safe." So I got up early, around 4:00 in the morning, and took the teenage girls, and we walked all the way to Duala.

The rebel soldier was so vexed when he came back the next day and we were gone. But we were safe. And he couldn't have my girl. My father had a safe place for my girls in Duala.

When things were a bit safer, we came home to Jesus Christ Children's Ministry. But soon came the big war. We called it World War IV. And so I got more children. I started taking in boys too, and so I had two boys and twenty-nine girls.

But the day came when we had no food and were so hungry. The children would go out into the bush and gather sour plums to eat. They took my dishpan and would gather it full. When they would bring it back to me, I would add a little sugar. They loved to drink it like juice because they were so hungry. Every other hour or so they would go get the sour plums, and I would fix it for them to drink.

But of course we were still hungry. Then I heard the news that rice was cheap in Duala, so I knew I needed to go there and get rice for my children. I got up early in the morning and took some of my children with me to go get the rice. We saw the dissidents everywhere we went. And they would command us, "Line up—everyone line up!"

Then they would ask, "Where you from?"

And we would say, "We from right here." Never would you say from Taylor's land, or they would shoot you dead.

I bought bulgur wheat, rice, bony fish, and split peas. The rice was so cheap because they had looted the port. We gathered our bags and left. I knew all the soldiers would want rice more than bulgur wheat. So I put a big bag of bulgur wheat on my head and small bags of rice on my children's heads. And I commanded them to walk and not look or answer to anyone. I knew the rebel soldiers would check my bags, but if the children looked like vagabond children who were orphaned or abandoned, maybe the soldiers would just ignore them. And I refused to even give them one cup of our rice. Because I knew what

happened to other people—they walked all the way to Duala to get rice, and when they came back to White Plains, the rebel soldiers would stop them, take all their rice, and let them go free. Free, but with nothing to eat. And we were getting into desperate times.

It worked. The rebels would check my bags, but they would just ignore my children. And my children walked straight. They didn't look to the right or left; they just obeyed me, went out ahead, and walked.

So we kept walking on that road. And as soon as we heard a sound, we would jump into the bush. For safety, we had to take another route so that my children could save the food and avoid the rebels who were on the road. But this meant we had to cross a big creek. We allowed the boys to cross first; the water was strong. And so I told the boy, "Look, Christopher, if the force is too strong, leave the rice." But he held on. He was fourteen years old, and he knew how to swim.

God helped us. The rebels did not take any of our food, but they took everything else in the whole area; they ate all the chickens and dogs.

But we continued to struggle. We put rice in the bulgur wheat to stretch it. And life was not easy. I was still struggling even after the war finally ended. I would wake up in the morning and pray, "Lord, help me find something today for these children to eat."

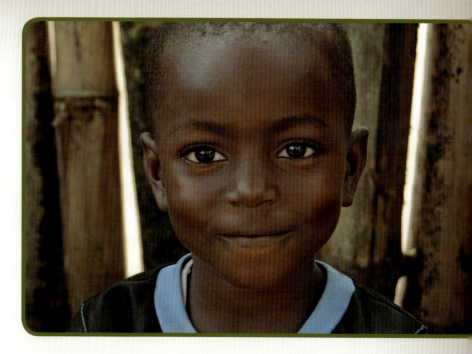

I learned about Christian Aid, and they helped me a bit, but not on a regular distribution. It was July 23, 2007, when I called them in desperation. And they said that the food distribution program that had been helping me was unable to give anything at the time. The only thing they were helping with was tools for farmers.

And I just didn't know what to do; I was at the point of desperation. I had twenty-nine children, and even though the war was over, we needed help. We needed food. Our school needed funding. So I got all of my team members to pray along with me. And then, right after I finished praying, my phone rang. It was James Yoder, the director for the orphan program at Christian Aid. He told me he wants to meet with me.

INSIDE THE BAMBOO WALLS | 95

At that meeting James told me he would put us on the Christian Aid program, which meant we would get food, clothes, and help for our school. Regular help, every month. Oh, we celebrated that day so much! We sang and our praise and worship was so lively—we were just celebrating. Our tough times were finally over, and we were praising God for that.

And today I have my home, a home for boys and girls. We have a school right here, across the road from my home in the bamboo walls. After school the boys play football (soccer) and the girls play their African children's games of Lapa and Parker Pea. Or they plait hair or work on their homework. They are happy, and they are loved. And my older girls love to go to CAM's youth retreat, and last year they almost didn't go because it was right after Suah died. But then they decided to go anyway, and they sang this song: "What a Friend We Have in Jesus." They won a prize for singing it. And I was so happy they won that prize because that song means so much to us here at this home.

Isaiah 50:7, "For the Lord GOD will help me; therefore shall I not be confounded: therefore have I set my face like a flint, and I know that I shall not be ashamed," is the verse we have on the wall of our orphanage, and it's the verse we live by. And at night I have devotions with my children, and I tell them that it is only because of Jesus we survived that awful war. And it is because of Him that we have food and clothes today.

And for me, I know it's because of Jesus that my children love me and call me "ma." And it's because of Jesus that I can keep helping the children of Jesus Christ Children's Ministry.

> For the Lord GOD will help me;
>
> therefore shall I not be confounded:
>
> therefore have I set my face like a flint,
>
> and I know that I shall not be ashamed.

CHAPTER EIGHTEEN
A REASON TO SMILE AGAIN

SOMETIMES YOU HEAR babies crying from their *lapas* on their mothers' backs. Sometimes you see them crawling around on the filthy dirt of their front yard. Sometimes you see them laughing and smiling just like all little babies in the world.

And sometimes they are so quiet you are afraid they are on the verge of leaving this life forever.

But we find hope. Hope for the mothers, hope for the babies—hope for the nations.

Back a long, rutted road in Ganta, Nimba County, sits a feeding center for malnourished babies. This feeding center is part of Hope for the Nations, a Canadian-based organization that also supports a school and a child sponsorship program in the area.

At the feeding center, hope comes in the form of crumbled moringa leaves. They have a menu tacked on the wall: Breakfast—powder mixed with honey and one cup of milk, Benemix. Lunch—Benemix with rice porridge, moringa powder mixed with honey and one cup of milk. Supper—rice with any sauce, one cook spoon of moringa powder added to the sauce.

Moringa is a multipurpose tropical tree, easy to grow, with leaves rich in proteins, vitamins, and minerals. It has become widely used in projects fighting against malnutrition.[1] The leaves have a whopping seven times the vitamin C of oranges; four times the vitamin A of carrots; four times the calcium of milk, and three times the potassium of bananas.[2]

Hope for the Nations provides the feeding center with funds and

---

1 Sanford Holst, *Moringa: Nature's Medicine Cabinet*, 2d ed., (Los Angeles: Santorini Publishing, 2011), p. 13.

2 Ibid., p. 12.

supplies. However, they have no steady source of nutritional milk, so Christian Aid Ministries helps provide milk for the tiny babies as it is available. Mothers from Liberia and Guinea bring their malnourished babies to the center for help. Mary Ann Newah, the feeding center director, helps the mothers feed their babies and demonstrates how to take care of them. The tiny ones get milk, and the older ones get nutritious food mixed with moringa leaves. The mothers stay and care for their babies at the center until they are strong enough to go home again.

Sennie Kparmie has a little boy at Hope for the Nations. She is from Guinea, so she doesn't even speak English. We sat in the darkness, flashlights in hand, and talked through a translator. She told us her story.

"My first three children I had with a man who then left me because I was crippled. I was not perfect for him.

"And now my little Mesa—he be one year and two months old now. But when he was nine months old, his body just started to drop down. And the people in my community told me to stop feeding him, that my milk was not good anymore.

"And every time I fed Mesa, he would vomit. So I stopped breast-feeding him and began to give him real food. He was nine months old, so I thought he is old enough for this. But his body just started to drop down. I did not know what to do.

"The little boy's grandmother, she said he needs help. So she tied a black rope around his neck and waist. She said this will help him to recover faster. Then some people told me to take him to Hope Village. They said, 'Look, Sennie, go to Hope Village. Take your baby there, and he will survive.'

"So I came all the way from Guinea to Hope Village. And the people here, oh, they are helping me plenty! My baby Mesa is surviving. He is eating rice and is doing so much better.

"When I came, the lady in charge asked what the ropes were for. So I told her why the boy's grandmother put them on him. And she said, 'Well, if these were supposed to save your child, why did you bring him to Hope Village?' I didn't know what to say. So the lady destroyed them.

"And my baby continued to get better. He is not completely well yet, so we will stay awhile longer until he is healthy and I don't have to worry anymore that he will die.

"I felt so bad, so bad, when my baby was so sick—like I was the one to blame or something. But now that I see he will survive, that he will not die, I can just always be singing songs. I have a reason to smile again.

"And when I go home and see other babies who are dropping down and reducing, I will tell them to go. Go to Hope Village—the people there, they care. They will help you."

It was late, and the mosquitoes were buzzing around us. Sennie needed to go put her baby Mesa to bed. But she had one more thing to tell me.

"Here, I have a reason to smile again. My baby will survive. But when I go back home, I am afraid. Maybe my second man will also leave me, because I am not beautiful. I am crippled. And I will be alone again."

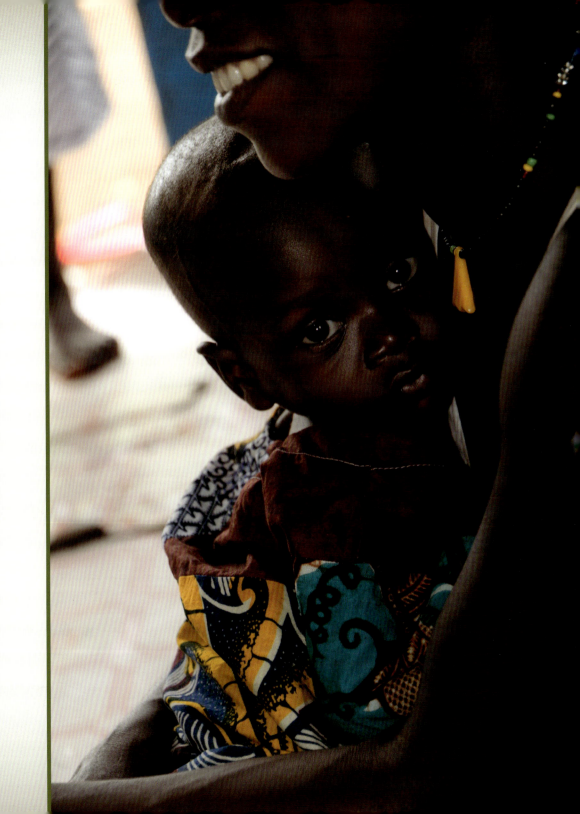

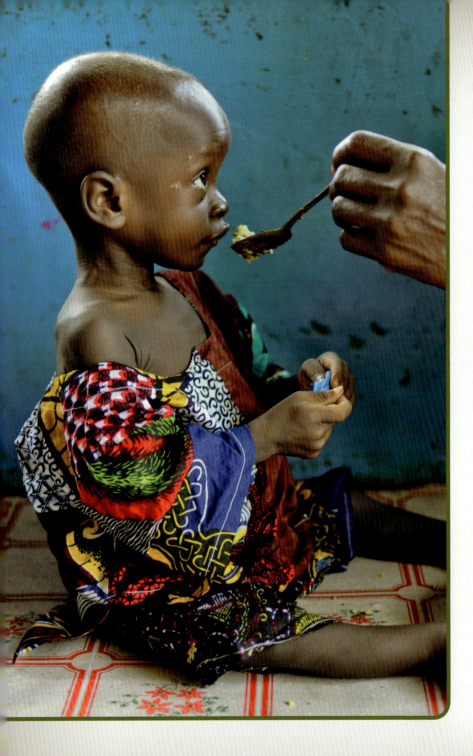

The words hung in the black of the night, and somewhere deep inside of me something resonated over the cultural and language barriers. Here, she had a reason to smile again. She was enough for her baby; because of her care for him and help from Hope for the Nations, little Mesa was thriving.

But at home, she wasn't good enough. So her gratitude for life was mixed with memories of a painful past, and the redemption of her little boy was shadowed by the fear of rejection in the future.

Maybe I am not beautiful enough. I'm not perfect.

Mary Ann and I hugged Sennie and told her that Jesus is perfect and can make her beautiful and whole on the inside. I told her I love her and that Jesus won't turn her away because she's not perfect on the outside.

When we left the next day, it was pouring rain. We dashed to the Land Cruiser and waved goodbye through windows streaming with water. The story is over.

Yet it's not—because someday the perfect will come!

But when that which is perfect is come, then
that which is in part shall be done away.
—1 CORINTHIANS 13:10

CHAPTER NINETEEN
A FEARFUL THING

"IT'S JUST GOD who can help the children survive. Sometimes they come and we just don't know if they will live or not. So we pray and pray and pray. And it is so fearful; we don't know if the babies will survive." –Mary Ann Newah

When you hold one of the malnourished children in your arms and coax her to take a bite of rice, it's so different from just looking at photos of her. Death seems a real possibility. And it's a fearful thing, just like Mary Ann says. When she tells me she prayed for a child to survive, I know it wasn't a prayer said in passing, such as, "Please, God, help the baby get better soon." It was the kind of prayer born from a desperate heart that knows the only way the child will survive is if God steps in with His healing and helps the child open her mouth and eat.

I tried to help an severely malnourished little girl eat some rice. She was four years old and could hardly even walk. Every rib and bone in her body seemed to poke out at sharp angles. Her name was Myra. When she was two years old, she got sick, and ever since that she has had no appetite. None.

We tried to get her to eat. Painstakingly, she would. Every grain of rice that made it into her mouth was cause for celebration—something so basic, yet so vital. It tore my heart apart.

I sat on a broken piece of block beside Ole Ma Martha, a caretaker for the babies at the feeding center. We coaxed Myra to eat one tiny bite, and then another. She did eat, but only a minute amount. She was simply too weak and tiny. I don't know if the food will even stay in her stomach. I think she has chronic diarrhea. It really is a fearful thing. And Myra is only one of so many hurting and malnourished children in Africa.

But every story is different. Every child is special. When I saw Myra, I could picture how Hawa, another little girl I met at the feeding center, must have looked when she arrived.

When Hawa was born, the people all said, "What, can a dead body give birth to a child?" Her mother was terribly sick when she gave birth, and everyone said Hawa was born half dead.

Hawa's mother died in childbirth, and her father brought Hawa to Hope for the Nations. There, Mary Ann put her into an incubator. Her father asked, "Can she live?" Ole Ma Martha remembers she was breathing, but the blanket covering her chest didn't even move.

It took some time, but after three months Hawa began to make a little progress, and now she is a healthy little girl. She drank a lot of CAM-donated milk. God reached out His healing hand and through the milk helped her grow.

Hawa became best of friends with

another one of Ole Ma Martha's charges, a charming little boy named Bobbyson.

Bobbyson's story is exceptionally heartbreaking; even Mary Ann, who has seen so much pain and heartache, says so. When we saw Bobbyson, he was a bit of a rebel, but a lovable one. Although he could act like a big bully occasionally, it was all bluff. When you looked into his eyes, you saw it was just that impish little boy spirit.

Bobbyson's mother was a Muslim. In Liberia, tribal ties go very deep. It's okay for a Muslim man to marry a Gio or Mano girl, but this was different. This was a Muslim girl who married a Gio man. So when Bobbyson was born, his mother's father was furious and wanted to get rid of the child. He decided the best way would be for the boy to simply get sick and die on his own—so he controlled and manipulated his daughter to the extent that Bobbyson did not receive proper care and feeding. He became severely malnourished.

Eventually Bobbyson's father left his mother and brought Bobbyson to Hope for the Nations. At that time the boy looked fat. Sometimes malnourishment makes children wither away and leaves just a bit of skin with a lot of ribs and bones. But sometimes it's the other way—the whole body shuts down, the kidneys stop functioning, and the child becomes bloated. It is not a good sort of chubby; it's horrible.

Bobbyson thrived at Hope for the Nations. He was Ole Ma Martha's little charge, and she loved him so much. But his mother still wanted Bobbyson, even though she had neglected him earlier. She would come and hang around the compound and try to sneak him away, but Martha would have nothing of it. She said, "I can't give Bobbyson to you, because you almost killed him. And soon he will be like a friend to me." What she meant was that Bobbyson had stolen his way into her heart.

His mother never managed to take him. But the day came when Bobbyson's father

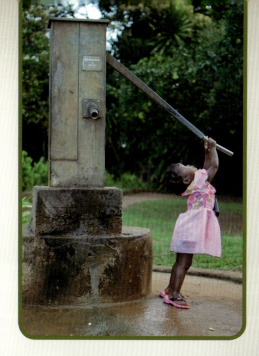

A FEARFUL THING | 105

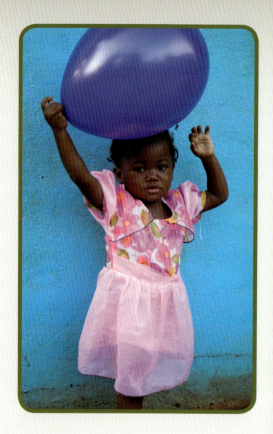

came to take him. He wanted Bobbyson to come live with him.

But Bobbyson didn't want to leave Martha, whom he thought of as his ma. Martha told us that when they came for him, he was hanging onto her *lapa*. He didn't want to go.

When she told me the story, she ended with, "Anywhere I could go, Bobbyson, he would just follow me. I cried when he left."

What will the rest of Bobbyson's life hold? Will his dad care for him? Will his mother try to use him to get back together with her former husband? Will his dad get another woman, and will she love Bobbyson? Will he be able to fit in anywhere if he is part Muslim and part Gio? I don't know. But I do know he was loved once. Martha truly cared for him.

And the fearful thing became a wonderful thing—Bobbyson was rescued from starvation.

I gave Martha the picture of Bobbyson playing at the feeding center, standing by the doorway. I'm sure she treasures it. As an ole ma who raised eight children herself, she not only cares for many more children, but also loves them with all her heart. She testifies, "He became my friend; and oh, when we see the child survives, we know it is just God who did it."

106 | SOME KIND OF LOVE

CHAPTER TWENTY
A DIFFERENT ENDING

I AM THE face of a child in Liberia, West Africa.

I live at an orphanage, but I can't claim the title of *orphan*—because I'm not that. I can't say my parents died, because they didn't. They abandoned me.

Some of the other children at the orphanage are actually orphans, so to keep things simple, we are all called orphans. Ma and Pa Beh is what we call the director and his wife. They started this orphanage during the war, in 1996. They love us and take good care of us here.

Some of my friends here are Jesse and Jessica. They used to live at a different orphanage, but something terrible happened there, so they came to live with us. A lot of witchcraft happened at their orphanage. The directress was a wicked woman, and she found out that she could get a lot of money if she would sacrifice a child. So she helped make a plan, and one night a small boy was sent out to buy a small biscuit for 10 LD (about 15 cents USD). Another child went with him, and they were both captured that night. And they were sacrificed—their bodies were mutilated, and their fingers, toes, and eyes were cut out. And all of that was sold for 1200 USD.

So the Ministry of Health found out about this, and they shut down the orphanage. They brought Jesse and Jessica to live here.

Another one of my friends is Kehbi. She is a big girl now, because she was the first baby brought to the orphanage. Kehbi was born in the interior of Liberia, in Number 5 District of Grand Bassa County. When she was about a week old, her mother went to the village creek for water, but she didn't come back. The other villagers went to find her, but all they saw was her bucket by the creek bank. They never heard anything more from her again, so Kehbi needed to go live somewhere else.

Ma and Pa Beh love us and take good care of us. They make sure babies who come to the orphanage get the right kind of food to eat. They buy benne seed for the babies once they get a little older, and they prepare it by beating it to dust in a pestle and mortar. The babies grow and stay healthy with the nutritious food.

My friend Morris came to the orphanage when he was only a baby. Sometimes Ma Beh calls him Number Fourteen, because Morris was his mother's fourteenth child. His mother had a sad life because only seven of her children survived. And then she died when Morris was born.

So they brought him to the orphanage when he was only one day old, and he survived. And that is so good because lots of babies outside this orphanage just die if their mother dies, because no one takes care of them and makes sure they get the right kind of food to eat.

So we all live here at the orphanage together, with unfortunate beginnings to our life stories.

But Mardea tells me we can be different and choose to make our lives better. She grew up at the orphanage, and she's still here. She just turned twenty-three, and she is a big sister to all of us children here at the orphanage. She's still going to school and doing lessons when she can. She's not popular at school because she does what's right. When they have "color day" at school, which is the day they don't have to wear their uniforms, the teachers tell her to help them monitor and make sure the girls wear decent clothes. So she helps out that way.

And she loves us a lot, especially the ones the others pick on. Like Conjay, the little boy who was brought here when he was just two

> Can a woman forget her sucking child, that she should not have compassion on the son of her womb? yea, they may forget, yet will I not forget thee. Behold, I have graven thee upon the palms of my hands.
>
> —ISAIAH 49:15-16A

days old. The children don't all like him; they say he is ugly and has a big mouth. But Mardea loves him anyway, and because she shows him love, he does well during devotions and always knows his Bible verse and sings loudly.

My only possessions are a backpack, a Bible, a teddy bear, a spoon, a blanket, and a bunk in a room with twenty other boys.

I am a child in Africa—one of many, but I have my own story.

These are the children of Africa, some orphaned, some abandoned, but all with a set of misfortunes straight from the beginning of their lives. More than anything, I want them to live in a better world—a world of love and care and discipline so that they can have a different ending to their stories.

If I could tell them only one thing, I would try to impress on them how much they mean to God. I would say, "Your name is etched on God's hands. He cares about you. In His Word He even says that if your mother would forsake you, He never will. And I know that happened to some of you. Your own mother may have deserted you, but Jesus promised He never would."

I would also tell them, "God cares about you so much that He

A DIFFERENT ENDING | 111

gives you a choice. He wants you to choose to leave behind the stigma of the words *orphan, underprivileged, abandoned, unwanted*—these words that were part of your story ever since you were just a tiny child.

"Jesus can change you. He can give you a different ending to the sad start in your story. But you have to choose to let Him. I can't force you. A relief agency can't force you. Even your directress can't force you.

"But you can choose how your story will end."

We all need to choose. No matter where or how we began, no matter what our current situation, the choice is ours.

The choice to overlook a hurt. The choice to go on even when it seems impossible. The choice to love God with all our heart and soul, and then do what He wants us to do. The choice to go where He calls us, even when it's not where we want to go. The choice to forgive, to risk and love and commit. The choice to show compassion. The choice to live abundantly.

Those choices are in our hands.

I call heaven and earth to record this day against you, that I have set before you life and death, blessing and cursing: therefore choose life, that both thou and they seed may live: That thou mayest love the LORD thy God, and that thou mayest obey his voice, and that thou mayest cleave unto him: for he is thy life, and the length of thy days.
DEUTERONOMY 30:19-20a

112 | SOME KIND OF LOVE

APPENDIX:
REPORTS ON SELECTED NEEDS IN LIBERIA

EDUCATIONAL

An Educational Vision

AGRICULTURAL

An Axe, a Cutlass, and a Paring Knife

MEDICAL

A Bundle Can Save a Baby's Life

EDUCATIONAL NEEDS IN LIBERIA

AN EDUCATIONAL VISION

- According to a UNICEF report, the largest out-of-school population is in sub-Saharan Africa, where around 29 million children of primary school age are out of school.[1] Liberia, West Africa, lies in this sub-Saharan region.

- In Liberia, a child generally is forced to share his textbook with up to twenty-seven other children, while in America each child has five or six of his own textbooks.

- About 40 percent of Liberians cannot read or write their own name. Simply stated, 2 out of 5 Liberian people are illiterate.[2]

---

1 "Basic Education and Gender Equality," September 16, 2011, <http://www.unicef.org/education/bege_59826.html>, accessed on January 24, 2013.

2 *The World Factbook 2013*, Washington, DC: Central Intelligence Agency, 2013, <https://www.cia.gov/library/publications/the-world-factbook/geos/li.html>, accessed on January 28, 2013.

FROM STATISTICS TO REALITY

Interested in finding out more about Liberian education, several of us visited schools in Buchanan, Grand Bassa County. We found teachers who were doing their best with the little they had, but several things concerned us.

At times, teachers did not seem to have a good grasp of the subject matter, and their students were taught erroneously. For instance, we saw spelling words on a chalkboard for the children to study, but some were misspelled. Children are taught solely by repetition and rote learning, so what is spelled on the board is what they will learn. Their assignments/lessons are simply the words the teacher writes on the board, copied directly to their copybooks.

At a school at one of the orphanage homes, children tried to study in a makeshift shelter. Their old school had been made of mud blocks and had crumpled to the ground, and the new one was still in the building process. Through the torrential downpours of rainy season, this was a major problem. CAM provided copybooks for each orphan child on the program, but there was no way to keep them dry. Many of the children did not even bring their copybooks to school. Only one teacher was present that day, and he was trying to control a classroom of eighty-three children. Teaching one concept to multiple grades does not work well; only about 25 percent of the children could see the letters and numbers the teacher was writing on the chalkboard.

A VISION FOR SUSTAINABILITY

At the time of this writing, CAM is supporting 1,530 children at 42 orphanages, and 966 children in church guardian homes. Each child receives approximately 40 pounds of food each month, including rice, sugar, beans, flour, and oil. The orphanage children attend sponsored schools at the orphanages, while the church guardian children have all their school fees paid. CAM also helps with emergency medical complications and other needs for the orphans on the program.

While these needs continue, sustainability must also be addressed. The children of Liberia need better education, especially in the remote areas. This need provides an opportunity for godly training to take place. During their summer breaks, national teachers could be trained intensively in subjects such as phonics, and school infrastructure could be developed.

Many children do want to study and learn, and steps must be taken to help them do so. Teachers are doing the best they can with the resources available, but they could do so much more with good training and supplies. Even though the needs are overwhelming, with vision and perseverance there is hope for Liberian education. The purpose of education is to enable students

to serve their Creator with all their potential. A better education, coupled with the knowledge of Christ and the desire to follow Him, will provide a better future for the children and culture of Liberia. The teachers of the orphanage schools can be empowered to teach in a way that will influence their students to accept Christ into their lives, making the next generation dynamic disciples for Him.

Most of the things worth doing in this world have been declared impossible before they were done.
–L. BRANDEIS

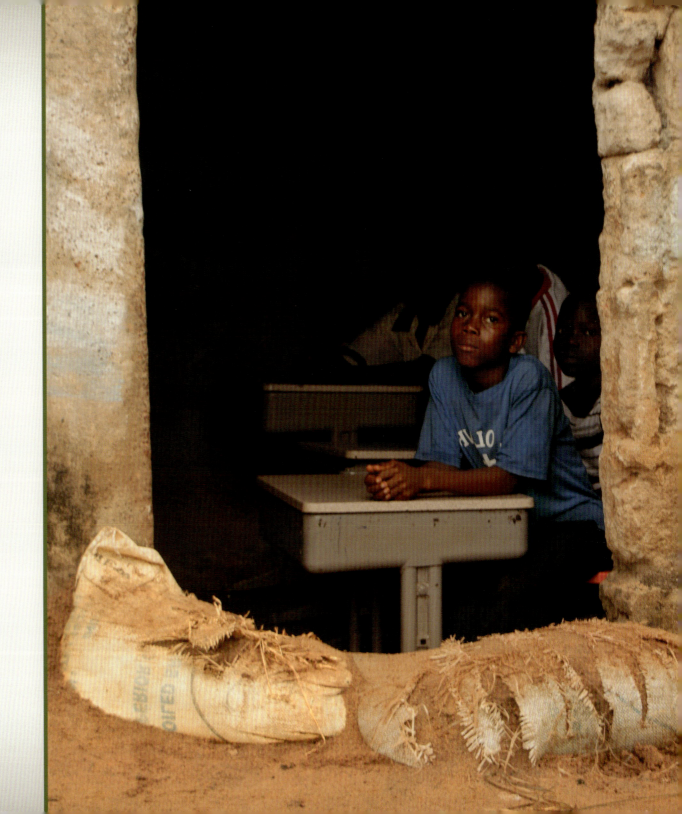

AGRICULTURAL NEEDS OF LIBERIA

AN AXE, A CUTLASS, AND A PARING KNIFE

FROM STATISTICS TO REALITY

Rice and *what's for dinner* are synonymous in Liberia. You may ask someone if he's eaten yet that day, and even if he has consumed a lot of bread or other food but no rice, he will say, "I ain't ate yet." Rice is the word. It's the staple food, but it does not come free or without problems.

If rice imports were suddenly cut off, most of Liberia would suffer. A diminished rice supply would bring havoc to the whole country, but especially to the people living in the city of Monrovia. This city is extremely overcrowded since the war—it was built for 550,000, and now there are 1.4 million people living in it. Here are a few statistics to show the shaky economic situation of rice and agriculture in Liberia.

- Nearly all Liberians eat a large bowl of rice every day—about one cup of rice per person.

- That means 3 million cups of rice (30,000 bags) are consumed every day in Liberia.

- Only 40 percent of Liberia's rice is grown in the country; the rest is imported from Asia and South America.[1]

- A ship can carry 400,000 bags of rice.

This means that most of Liberia's main source of food is imported, despite the fact that the land in Liberia could easily supply enough rice for the entire country if it would be developed and used to grow rice.

---

1 *The Situation of Children and Women in Liberia 2012: From Conflict to Peace* (UNICEF), p. 32.

RICE HARVEST

So we ask, why isn't more rice grown in the country? Several reasons exist. First, Liberia's two main staple crops, rice and cassava, are grown by subsistence farmers. These farmers usually sell their surplus produce immediately after the harvest to settle their debts, and seed rice is not saved for the next planting. Also, rice is not the easiest crop to grow and harvest.

I went with a group to visit a rice farm at Disco Hill, Margibi County, Liberia. There we met Alfred and Hegins. Alfred is the farmer. He is a man from Bomi County, and he only came to this area after the war. A Bassa woman lent him the land for his rice farm. Hegins is a Ghanaian man who works on some Christian Aid Ministries agriculture projects.

We walked through the swamp to Alfred's rice farm. The best-yielding rice is what is grown right in the swamp, but the women were harvesting the rice on the hillside when we were there.

To start the rice farm, Alfred and two of his young friends cleared this land. First they had to fell the large trees with an axe. After testing the soil, they cleared the land by cutting the weeds with a cutlass and burning the brush. Then it took fourteen days to work up the soil, using only the primitive hand tools of scratching hoes.

In the springtime, before rainy season begins, Alfred plants his rice. It grows during rainy season, and then harvest begins in October. The ladies were in the fields harvesting the rice when we visited. They do it all by hand, simply breaking the tops of the stalks and gathering them in their hands. If the rice stalks are still green, Alfred uses a paring knife to cut them off. When the stalks are dry enough, they stomp on them with their feet to remove the grains of rice.

The rice is then laid out to dry in the sunshine. If the rain is too heavy during that time, they parch it over a fire.

Next the ladies beat the rice in a mortar to loosen the chaff from the actual grains of rice. Then they "fan the rice" to remove the chaff from the grains.

That is rice harvest.

Hegins and Alfred shared slightly varying viewpoints. Hegins shakes his head at what he views as a poor work ethic in the people of Bassa. He said, "I been here fourteen years now; I know these people! You give them a cutlass, they will sell it; you give them seed rice, they will eat it!"

But Alfred, who has farmed this land since the war, was

discouraged. He said, "My family, we need to eat. I know we should save the seed rice—I want to save it for seed rice—but we need to eat. We need to survive. If I harvest it, we will need to eat it, because there is not enough to last us through all of dry season."

Hegins tried to encourage him. "Alfred, don't give up hope. Save the seed rice by selling more vegetable. Grow more vegetable, then you will be able to buy rice for your family, and save this for seed rice, for a bigger crop next year. When the Christian Aid people come again, they will see your kitchen foot (full) with seed rice! Don't give up hope. We will see what God can do for you, yeah? Don't give up hope."

FARMING CHALLENGES

Growing rice is hard work, and Alfred is not the only farmer in Liberia who struggles daily. Challenges for farmers in Liberia include the following:

- Limited access to quality supplies (e.g. seeds and fertilizers)[2]
- Pests that destroy crops, such as groundhogs and insects[2]
- Poor roads and market infrastructure[2]

---

2   Florence A. Chenoweth et al., *The State of Food and Nutrition Security in Liberia: Comprehensive Food Security and Nutrition Survey 2010*, p. 5.

APPENDIX | 125

- No power saws, chainsaws, stump grinders, tractors, or bulldozers available[3]
- No modern farming techniques—ALL is done by hand[3]
- Considerable price pressure favoring cheap strains of imported rice, with which the local producers cannot compete[3]
- Poisonous snakes, malaria, parasites, yellow fever, and river blindness flies

After working hard to clear a patch of bush, farmers must wait several years to plant the second crop of rice—soil nutrients must be built up again.

Farmers also grow other crops that are not as difficult to produce:

- Potato greens (tops of sweet potatoes)
- Cassava
- Peppers
- Eggplant
- Okra
- Bananas
- Plantains

---

[3] *The Situation of Children and Women in Liberia 2012: From Conflict to Peace* (UNICEF), p. 33.

Most Liberian produce comes from the bush and is transported from the interior to the city. Another food source that comes from the bush is meat. Liberians eat any sort of animal that moves: birds, goats, dogs, cats, snakes, and monkeys. (They also eat pig feet and chicken feet.) But the transport of meat and vegetables is difficult due to poor roads, overloaded trucks, and many vehicle accidents.

DEVELOPING AGRICULTURE

Developing Liberia's potential in agriculture is important because it is imperative to Liberia's agricultural independence. The country's heavy dependence on rice imports creates a risk that the collapse or inflation of the market would put the entire country in desperate straits.

Here are practical ways to help the farmers of Liberia today:

I. Providing tool banks
   A. Shovels
   B. Axes
   C. Scratching hoes
   D. Cutlasses
   E. Picks
   F. Wheelbarrows
   G. Watering cans

II. Giving seeds/plants and fertilizer
   A. Seed rice
   B. Fertilizer
   C. Plantain and banana suckers
   D. Vegetable seeds and cassava sticks (starts)

III. Buying harvests
   A. Seed rice
   B. Cassava sticks

IV. Developing agriculture workshops
   A. Recover lost farming practices
   B. Combine agricultural and Biblical teaching
   C. Provide literature
   D. Teach sustainability
   E. Encourage Biblical work ethic
   F. Teach the Liberian people to regain community

Helping farmers with simple tools and knowledge of farming will allow Liberians to rely on rice and vegetables grown in their own country. Combining agricultural teaching with Biblical principles will help them to trust God as well, for He said,

So shall my word be that goeth forth out of my mouth: it shall not return unto me void, but it shall accomplish that which I please, and it shall prosper in the thing whereto I sent it.
—ISAIAH 55:11

128 | SOME KIND OF LOVE

MEDICAL NEEDS OF MOTHERS AND CHILDREN IN LIBERIA

A BUNDLE CAN SAVE A BABY'S LIFE

- Today, about 800 women will die worldwide in childbirth or from pregnancy-related complications.[1]

- Of the 190+ countries in the world, Liberia ranks seventh for maternal deaths.[2]

- In Liberia, the chance of dying in childbirth is 1 chance in 24, while in America it is only 1 chance in 2,400.[3]

---

[1] "Child Info: Monitoring the Situation of Children and Women," June 2012, <http://www.childinfo.org/maternal_mortality_overview.html>, accessed on April 19, 2013.

[2] "Child Info: Monitoring the Situation of Children and Women," June 2012, <http://www.childinfo.org/maternal_mortality_indicators.php>, accessed on April 19, 2013.

[3] Ibid.

AN ESSENTIAL CLINIC IN THE BUSH

I visited the Jacob Larety Town Clinic in February 2012. This clinic is located in Grand Bassa County, the county that rates the highest in all of Liberia for childbirth deaths.

The Jacob Larety Town Clinic serves eighty-six surrounding villages. Even in this modern age, you can't drive a car to the clinic. You can take a taxi from the city to the river, where you cross in a dugout canoe. From there, a five-minute hike will take you to the clinic.

Under a thatch-roofed market hut, I held babies and talked to Tamba, the OIC (Officer in Charge) for Jacob Larety Town Clinic. He told me how mothers—and often their babies—perish because they don't have access to medical care, and their attendants

APPENDIX | 131

(traditional midwives) are ill-trained to deal with any complications. Many of these deaths, brought on by obstructed labor, hemorrhaging, and postpartum sepsis, are totally preventable.

Distance hinders many women from coming to Tamba's clinic to have their babies, but culture and tradition hinder many more. Traditional midwives pressure women to have their babies in the village. The women agree because it has always been done this way.

But these traditional midwives use obsolete and atrocious practices, and sometimes things go wrong. Tamba said he heard how one midwife, when a baby was born and wasn't breathing, blew cigarette smoke into the baby's mouth and nose to try to get it to breathe.

In the two and a half years Tamba has been practicing at the clinic, he has heard of seven childbirth deaths in the nearby area. Many of these deaths could have been prevented if the women had come to his clinic instead of going to the midwife in their village.

BABY BUNDLES

Tamba has an idea, an incentive for women to come to his clinic to have their babies. His incentive is something simple that can be donated to the clinic for the women: bundles that contain diapers, blankets, pins, socks, sleepers, and hats. Sounds simple, but to these Liberian women, it's so special, they just might break tradition and make the extra effort to come to the clinic to have their babies.

If the mothers come to the Jacob Larety Town Clinic, they have a much better chance of survival. And if they run into any problems, they are only five minutes from the river where there is a canoe, and a taxi on the other side that can take them to the nearest hospital.

While at Jacob Larety Town Clinic, I interviewed two women who had received baby bundles recently. I met Moima and her newborn son Samouka. Moima had been on her way to the clinic from deep in the bush, and she didn't quite make it to the clinic but delivered her baby on the way. Though her baby wasn't born at the clinic, Tamba still gave her a bundle for making the effort to come.

Kulah Angel was born a healthy, chubby baby just two and a half weeks before I visited the clinic. Her mother Nancy was thrilled with her baby bundle. Tamba told me they let Kulah Angel's mother choose her bundle. It was a small choice to make, but not insignificant. The bundle may have saved little Kulah Angel's life, having motivated Nancy to have her baby at the clinic.

Supplying baby bundles to clinics in Liberia is an ongoing need. Up to 2,000 baby bundles a year can be used at CAM-sponsored clinics alone to help the mothers who come to have their babies.

GIFTS THAT GROW

Baby bundles are not the only thing that can help the maternal mortality rate in Liberia to drop. Kirk's Prenatal Vitamins contain vitamins A, B, C, D, and K as well as iodine and iron, which are important for a mother's health before and after the birth of her baby.

APPENDIX | 133

Kirk's also produces Child Health and Growth Vitamins, which greatly improve the health of little children in Liberia. Tamba said these vitamins are valuable because they are not readily available anywhere in Liberia. They cannot be found even at the large government hospitals, which only stock cheap imitation drugs. In this country with such a high childbirth death rate, vitamins containing these essential nutrients are priceless.

Kirk's Prenatal Vitamins are only a tiny part of CAM's Gifts-That-Grow program in Liberia. The other medicines that come as a result of the program are also making a life-changing difference for hundreds of people with various needs. The staff at Jacob Larety Town Clinic tell us if it were not for their monthly supply of these vitamins, medicines, and other supplies, there is no way they could stay in operation.

In all of our giving, we can demonstrate Christ and His love.

That thy way may be known upon earth, thy saving health among all nations.
—PSALM 67:2

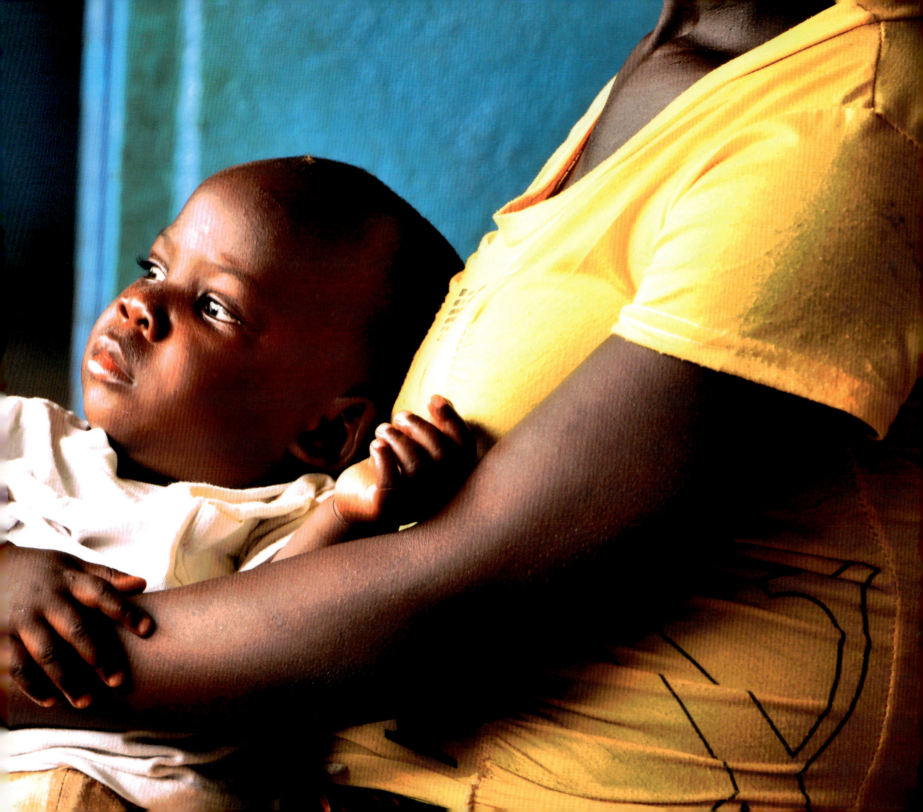

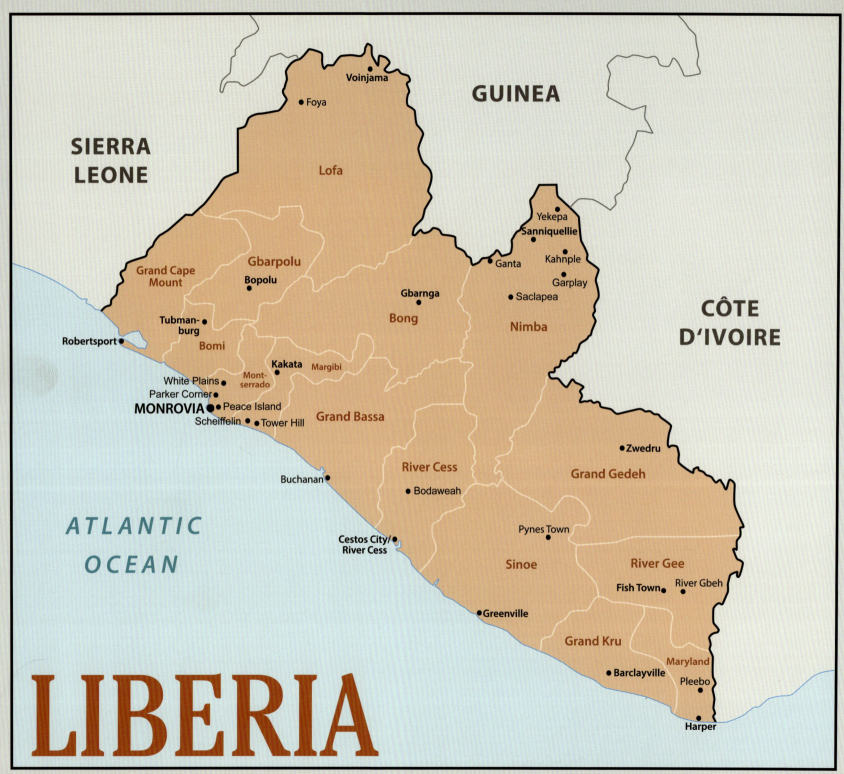

ABOUT THE AUTHOR & PHOTOGRAPHER

GLORIA MILLER worked as secretary for Christian Aid Ministries, a humanitarian aid organization, for six years. She spent two and a half of those years in Liberia, West Africa. This book contains her stories of malnourished and orphaned children. Gloria currently lives and works in Newcomerstown, Ohio. This is her first book.

MARCUS WILLEY, originally from Abbeville, South Carolina, directs the medical program for Christian Aid Ministries in Liberia, West Africa. This program supplies thirty-six clinics across Liberia with desperately needed medicines, free of charge. Marcus uses his photography skills to document the lives of the suffering people he comes across in his work in the medical field.

CHRISTIAN AID MINISTRIES

CHRISTIAN AID MINISTRIES was founded in 1981 as a nonprofit, tax-exempt 501(c)(3) organization. Its primary purpose is to provide a trustworthy and efficient channel for Amish, Mennonite, and other conservative Anabaptist groups and individuals to minister to physical and spiritual needs around the world. This is in response to the command ". . . do good unto all men, especially unto them who are of the household of faith" (Gal. 6:10).

Each year, CAM supporters provide approximately 15 million pounds of food, clothing, medicines, seeds, Bibles, Bible story books, and other Christian literature for needy people. Most of the aid goes to orphans and Christian families. Supporters' funds also help clean up and rebuild for natural disaster victims, put up Gospel billboards in the U.S., support several church-planting efforts, operate two medical clinics, and provide resources for needy families to make their own living. CAM's main purposes for providing aid are to help and encourage God's people and bring the Gospel to a lost and dying world.

CAM has staff, warehouse, and distribution networks in Romania, Moldova, Ukraine, Haiti, Nicaragua, Liberia, and Israel. Aside from management, supervisory personnel, and bookkeeping operations, volunteers do most of the work at CAM locations. Each year, volunteers at our warehouses, field bases, DRS projects, and other locations donate over 200,000 hours of work.

CAM's ultimate purpose is to glorify God and help enlarge His kingdom. ". . . whatsoever ye do, do all to the glory of God" (I Cor. 10:31).

THE WAY TO GOD AND PEACE

WE LIVE IN a world contaminated by sin. Sin is anything that goes against God's holy standards. When we do not follow the guidelines that God our Creator gave us, we are guilty of sin. Sin separates us from God, the source of life.

Since the time when the first man and woman, Adam and Eve, sinned in the Garden of Eden, sin has been universal. The Bible says that we all have "sinned and come short of the glory of God" (Romans 3:23). It also says that the natural consequence for that sin is eternal death, or punishment in an eternal hell: "Then when lust hath conceived, it bringeth forth sin: and sin, when it is finished, bringeth forth death" (James 1:15).

But we do not have to suffer eternal death in hell. God provided forgiveness for our sins through the death of His only Son, Jesus Christ. Because Jesus was perfect and without sin, He could die in our place. "For God so loved the world that he gave his only begotten Son, that whosoever believeth in him should not perish, but have everlasting life" (John 3:16).

A sacrifice is something given to benefit someone else. It costs the giver greatly. Jesus was God's sacrifice. Jesus' death takes away the penalty of sin for everyone who accepts this sacrifice and truly repents of their sins. To repent of sins means to be truly sorry for and turn away from the things we have done that have violated God's standards. (Acts 2:38; 3:19).

Jesus died, but He did not remain dead. After three days, God's Spirit miraculously raised Him to life again. God's Spirit does something similar in us. When we receive Jesus as our sacrifice and repent of our sins, our hearts are changed. We become spiritually alive! We develop new desires and attitudes (2 Corinthians 5:17). We begin to make choices that please God (1 John 3:9). If we do fail and commit sins, we can ask God for forgiveness. "If we confess our sins, he is faithful and just to forgive us our sins, and to cleanse us from all unrighteousness" (1 John 1:9).

Once our hearts have been changed, we want to continue growing spiritually. We will be happy to let Jesus be the Master of our lives and will want to become more like Him. To do this, we must meditate on God's Word and commune with God in prayer. We will testify to others of this change by being baptized and sharing the good news of God's victory over sin and death. Fellowship with a faithful group of believers will strengthen our walk with God (1 John 1:7).